IN DEFENSE OF DEMOCRACY

Companion books edited by Thomas H. Johnson

MEN OF TOMORROW
RETURN TO FREEDOM
A MAN'S REACH

IN DEFENSE

OF DEMOCRACY

EDITED WITH PREFATORY NOTES BY
Thomas H. Johnson

INTRODUCTION BY
Allan V. Heely

FOUNDED 1838

GPPS

G · P · PUTNAM'S SONS

NEW YORK

126516

CONTENTS

INTRODUCTION   vii
Allan V. Heely, The Lawrenceville School

THE OLD ORDER CHANGES   3
John J. McCloy, U.S. high commissioner for Germany

THE NEW ENVIRONMENT   21
Cord Meyer, Jr., president of the World Federalists

DON'T RESIGN FROM THE HUMAN RACE   35
Norman Cousins, editor of *The Saturday Review of Literature*

THE SHADOW OF COMMUNISM IN THE WESTERN WORLD   51
Arthur Sylvester, Washington correspondent, *The Newark Evening News*

EDUCATION FOR A NEW DEMOCRATIC ERA   63
Eduard C. Lindeman, Columbia University

ECONOMIC NATIONALISM AND WORLD TRADE   85
Charles W. Cole, president of Amherst College

SCIENCE SHAPES OUR LIVES   107
Detlev W. Bronk, president of The Johns Hopkins University

THE RELIGION OF JESUS AND THE DISINHERITED   125
Howard Thurman, pastor of the Fellowship Church, San Francisco

A LAYMAN LOOKS AT HIS WORLD   139
Lewis Perry, principal emeritus, Phillips Exeter Academy

INTRODUCTION

Education is an exercise in communication. It is man's effort, pursued by every means he can devise, to teach his young whence they came, where they are, what they can and ought to do about it; or, in more solemn language, to give them a knowledge of the past, an awareness of the present, a conscience toward the future. These are matters of concern to all people who hope to be useful. They give experience its meaning—a core to cleave to—and they are the main purpose of all teaching.

Concern for this purpose occupied the minds of the men who, some eight years ago, conceived the Lawrenceville Forum Lectures. The project was original: to present every year to the boys of the school men and women of distinction in various careers, and at intervals to publish their addresses in book form, both for their original audience and for the general public—communication first through present personality and later by the printed word. Lecturers were invited not merely to talk about their work, but more particularly to crystallize their experience into a statement of the problems young people would be called upon to face and of youth's responsibility for their solution. In advance of the formal addresses and afterward, whenever possible, opportunity was provided for informal conversations between boys and lecturers. This is the fourth volume in the Lawrenceville series.

INTRODUCTION

In meeting its obligations as an educational institution—as an instrument of communication—a school must attack on all fronts at once: through its formal curriculum, through athletics, through the whole gamut of its avocational resources, but most of all through teachers. For conviction and faith and hope and conscience—hard to come by and to hold, vague and elusive in the abstract—become present and attainable and impelling when they are exhibited by a vivid personality. Back of all effective teaching is a personality, whether the teacher be Socrates or Fagin. The little boy who says, "My father can lick your father," is not delivering a cool appraisal of pugilistic prowess; he is expressing, through masculine if vulgar metaphor, his conviction that he has been sired by a superior person, that is to say, a good teacher.

Great scholars, therefore, should be avoided by students unless they are also good teachers. For knowledge does not communicate itself through words alone, but only when it becomes incandescent in the minds and hearts of those who speak and hear it. College undergraduates, therefore, do well to elect men rather than courses. Garman affected the thinking of generations of Amherst men because he was a great personality, rather than because he was an academic philosopher; while Harvard's Kittredge and Yale's Phelps taught themselves through and in addition to their subject matter; and their fame is anecdotal rather than scholarly.

The lectures in this book are the work of men of distinction as publicists, teachers, or public servants. Their distinction was a prerequisite of their selection. But even more important, in the estimate of those responsible for choosing them, was the expectation that by virtue of their personalities—the way they looked and sounded, their knowledge and their ardor—through the magical potency of physical presence, leading the school to say, "These are the very people who have done these things," they would be able to shake their hearers loose from apathy, indifference, ignorance, and prejudice.

They did much to uproot apathy and indifference. All of them were listened to and discussed and appraised, and controversy over what they said was sometimes animated to the point of violence. Boys remembered them a long time afterward, too.

These men trod sturdily, also, on the toes of ignorance and prejudice. It is a memorable observation of Lord Peter Wimsey that "there's nothing you can't prove if your outlook is only sufficiently limited." Many of us Americans would rather be sure than be right. Ours is the dogmatism of little knowledge, the foolish faith that "easy does it." As the Private Journal of Amiel has it, "We like the attainment of the aim, not the pursuit of the aim, the goal, not the road, the idea that is ready-made, the bread that is ready-baked. . . . We desire conclusions." And so we jump at them, without looking to see how we got to them. There are those of us, therefore, who cannot tell what we think until we find out what our favorite newspaper columnist or radio commentator thinks. And then we think what they think, or what we think they think; and conversation about public affairs becomes the competitive bandying of unconsidered misquotations. The Lawrenceville lecturers broadened the outlook, gave mileposts to the thinking, sharpened the awareness of their hearers. There is ample evidence, also, not only that they raised questions and stimulated controversy, but that some of their audience have received light upon their path and a vision of their destination and of how it becomes a man to bear himself upon the journey.

In short, they have communicated—an art so difficult that few have mastered it. Here are teachers.

ALLAN V. HEELY

IN DEFENSE OF DEMOCRACY

John J. McCloy

JOHN J. MCCLOY belongs to that group of Americans for whom the opportunity to serve their country is always more compelling than the call to private profit. A graduate of the Harvard Law School, he has but intermittently been permitted to indulge in the practice of law. His association with official Washington began in 1940. For four years thereafter he gave distinguished service as Assistant Secretary of War. In 1947 he became president of the World Bank of the United Nations, a position he resigned in May, 1949, to become United States high commissioner for Germany.

What follows is in the nature of memoirs, covering principally the war years 1941–1945, of one highly placed participant. Some of its revelations and comments give a slant on men and events not to be found elsewhere in print.

T. H. J.

THE OLD ORDER CHANGES

by John J. McCloy

NEARLY HALF a century ago in 1900, Brooks
Adams published a really remarkably prophetic
book. It was called, *America's Economic Destiny*.
It pointed out the growing cracks in the old order, which
then seemed so secure, particularly the supremacy of Great
Britain and the potentialities for world leadership, which
he then saw as being implicit in the natural, industrial,
and human resources of the United States.

Now, four years after the end of the second great world
conflict, we see many of Brooks Adams's predictions ful-
filled. While other countries were devastated or bank-
rupted, America's productive plant has expanded, and the
volume of her trade has greatly increased. Her present pre-
eminence among the nations is unmatched in modern history. But most Americans can derive very little comfort or
sense of security from this fortunate status when we realize
that the fate of the country is irrevocably linked with that
of the rest of the world and that America's well-being cannot long be maintained amid growing misery and demorali-
zation abroad.

In this period of confusion and unrest it is time, I think,
to reassess our values, to try to reorient ourselves, and to
chart a course that will guide us through this very difficult
postwar period. During the war it was my fortune to have

been rather closely associated with a number of aspects of the military effort and more recently with those whose responsibility it is to rebuild a functioning world economy. I frequently have thought of what I could glean out of that experience which might be of value to guide us in meeting the difficult issues that lie ahead.

I saw, when I was in the War Department, most of the men who reached high prominence in the war, and I feel that I saw, or was a part of, or on the fringe of, most of the important decisions of the war. I came away convinced of the fact that the war was not a chess game with every move coolly calculated. It was, at best, a succession of calculated risks, each with far-reaching potential consequences, but none of which could be planned for in advance except in a most general way. The important thing to me was that the shape of the given decision was determined in such large measure by the instinct or the pattern of mind of the man who made it, rather than by his careful premeditation or by his precise analysis. Whether men responded well or ill to the sudden personal emergencies was entirely a matter of their personal reserves, reserves long since built up or long since wasted or dissipated.

Churchill's courage and eloquence in the early days of the war (and those were reserves worth twenty divisions) were already in existence and instinctive with him when he came into power. What impelled him to send the last armored divisions that he had in England when England was still under the threat of invasion, when he sent the last division—I think it was the Second Armored—down to Egypt in '41 was a pattern and a characteristic of boldness and wisdom; it certainly wasn't the result of shrewd and careful calculation. The sending of those divisions, as you

4

perhaps all realize, did preserve the balance in that area at a very critical time, long before the United States came in.

Another decision that was made under great stress, and again, made largely by Mr. Churchill, was the decision to hold back the R.A.F. fighter force when the German armies were sweeping across France. The pressures that were brought to bear against him at that point were terrific. The armies were wasting away; the charge was made that England wasn't doing her share, and one knew that what strength England had was largely concentrated in that fighter force. But the instinct to preserve it and bring it to bear at the point where it could do most good, which was over the Channel and over England, was a principle that Churchill recognized, and due to his strength of character, even when his own cabinet was trying to get him to release those forces. It is another indication of the strength of his natural reserves. And it's interesting that there are two expressions of his courage and his wisdom. It was the firmness on one hand to follow a principle when there was a great clamor for an easy change, and it was his boldness to alter the principle when most would decline it that proved his strength. It reminds me of a story about Churchill which I think that at least English peoples will enjoy. His courage in following or in disavowing a principle, I think, is beautifully exemplified by this story.

It seems that Mr. Churchill, when he makes his speeches, always writes them out. And if they deal, of course, with foreign affairs, he sends them, somewhat reluctantly, over to the Foreign Office to have them examined and criticized before he delivers them. He sent this one over to the Foreign Office, and one of what he conceived to be the greatest passages in his speech he had ended with the preposition "of," which, as you all so well know, is a horrendous thing to do. You should never end a sentence with a preposition. He sent the speech over to the Foreign Office, and the Foreign Office made no comment of substance whatsoever, but some Etonian sent back the manuscript with a little circle about the offending preposition and stuck it back up into its proper position in the sentence. That was the only comment that the Foreign Office made. This, of course, when it reached Downing Street, drove Churchill into an elegant fury. He immediately sat down and sent a note over to the Foreign Minister reading, "This is the type of arrant pedantry up with which I will not put!"

It would be difficult to imagine a decision more crucial, more personal, or more wearing, in view of the huge stakes and the great responsibility involved than the one made by General Eisenhower when he fixed the date for the attack on the Normandy beaches in 1944. He alone could make the decision, and in spite of all the great resources at his disposal, there were enormous uncertainties. Any failure of the delicate timing for the invasion might mean great disaster, a disaster which could wipe out at one stroke all of the agonizing effort and sacrifice of the months and years of preparation. Only at certain intervals were tidal conditions right for the attack. The day first set was rejected because of threatening weather. And on the next possible day, the forecasts were still most uncertain.

As a matter of fact, there was a gale blowing at Eisenhower's headquarters when, relying on his weather reports as to what the weather might be over the invasion beaches, he gave the word. If the attack were not launched on that day, it would have to be postponed for a long period. The uncertainties were enormous, but Eisenhower chose that day. You must bear in mind that it wasn't far from that invasion area that another armada, the Spanish Armada, had been completely destroyed by the weather (if not completely, the defeat was largely brought about by the weather). And it's very grim to record that on the next possible day—that is, June 19, I believe it was—the great three-day storm that destroyed the mulberries and the gooseberries, those great installations that were put there to substitute for harbors, took place. And, if the landings had been attempted on that occasion, it's almost certain that the result would have been disaster.

Another great decision, according to my view, was when the word was sent out from the War Department to stand and fight on Bataan. You all remember in the early days of the war the rather uncertain defense of Singapore, the loss of prestige of the Allied Nations in the Far East, the cataclysm at Pearl Harbor. Our prestige was running rather low when the Japanese armies landed in the Philippines and began to press the Allied Armies there—that is, the Philippine Army and the United States Army down on the Bataan Peninsula. Mr. Quezon, the then president of the Philippines, sent in word saying that he felt the time had come to declare the neutrality of the Philippines. He was supported in that by the word of the American commissioner at that time. He felt the situation was hopeless and that it was, under all circumstances, the best thing to do. Even the military commander at that time sent in word that he felt that the situation was hopeless and that if neutrality were declared and if it were respected by the Japanese it might be something that could be taken into account.

7

Well, that decision, that telegram, came into the War Department, and it was necessary to have an immediate decision. I think no man was more influential in that than my chief, Secretary of War Stimson. All that night the matter was debated. I think it was largely Mr. Stimson's influence, as I say, which caused the telegram to go out the next morning saying that in spite of all the difficulties so far as the United States was concerned the Philippine Army could do what Quezon thought it was desirable to do, but in spite of the difficulties on Bataan, the only thing for the United States Army to do was to stand and fight. That was a very difficult order to send because one could clearly see that it meant the death, or capture, or the wounding of many, many Americans. But I think no one would now question the noble stand that the armies made, including the Philippine Army, and I must say that Mr. Quezon immediately responded to that spirit by sending a telegram to President Roosevelt the next day affirming his loyalty to that decision, with the result as you know it. I think that, again, was a decision that required basic courage and personal reserves of strength of character that served the country well in time of need.

The decision of General MacArthur not to stand in Australia but to hold Port Moresby, cross the Owen-Stanley Range, and seize Buna was another decision that sent a thrill through the East. The decision to attack straight across the Pacific, to bypass Truk, to go straight to the Marianas, to seize Saipan and Tinian I think was another bold decision which embodied many possible hazards.

All these decisions were made by men, pretty much on the spur of the moment, without any chance to prepare or reconsider or think about the tactical or logistic situation.

8

They came as a result of the fact that by the time the decision was upon them they had the habit and the nature of making decisions and decisions that involved great courage and strength of will.

The point I'm really trying to make is that these decisions come upon you suddenly; these tests come upon you not on the retake but on the first exam. The strains may not be the strains or tests of war. They are tests that may come at any time, but unless at places like this and the places to which you will go from this, you have trained yourself to take the sometimes difficult and wise decision the chances are that when the decision comes you will not be equipped to handle it.

The interesting thing, also, is, as I look back on my experience in the war, how young, or relatively young and inexperienced the men seemed to be who were making these decisions. The leaders in the War Department when I first went there were not the men who then commanded in the field, with the exception of General Marshall. They were young assistants, majors and lieutenant colonels like Bradley, Lawton Collins, and Bedell Smith, and others who were mere paper carriers in the War Department when I first went down there. I remember an experience that I had shortly after I arrived in the War Department, which I believe is worth telling.

I went down to see General Marshall one day. It happened that a young man came in and went out again while we were talking, and he said, "Did you happen to notice that man?" I said that I hadn't really paid any attention to him, and he said, "Well, you should have, because he's fit to be a corps commander today."

Well, I'd always thought of corps commanders as Civil

War veterans with big beards, and I was rather shocked at that and I said, "What makes you say that?"

He said, "Well, I was down at Fort Knox some time recently, and I was listening to some of the lectures that were going on there, and there was a man that made an exposition there of a machine-gun problem and it was so clear—there were some new ballistics connected with it—and it was so expressive that he caught my attention, and I've been following him ever since. I brought him into the War Department, and I'm convinced that he's one of our leaders."

I didn't think much more about that, but I did follow his career from then. He disappeared for a while in Pearl Harbor just after the bombing, but he turned up on Guadalcanal; he commanded the corps that drove the last Japanese off Guadalcanal. He later took Cherbourg. He was the man in command at the vital spot at the Battle of Mortain, of which perhaps many of you have never heard. It is probably the greatest defensive battle in which American forces have ever been engaged. It was there that the block was thrown that permitted Patton to go through at Saint Lô while this man—and his name is Lawton Collins—was helping hold off the eight divisions of armor that Hitler himself had ordered to break up the American Army on that peninsula. Patton broke through. Collins later commanded one of the spearheads that finally closed the surrounding of the Ruhr. I suppose that so far as history records he's the greatest corps commander or one of the greatest corps commanders the United States has ever had.

An interesting feature about that, which in a moment I will digress to point out, is that it was his articulateness at this Fort Knox lecture room that first called the attention of Marshall to him. Although one may know how to do a thing, it is so often important that you know how to tell someone else to do it. I remember in college in one of the lecture rooms there was a Latin motto. As a matter of fact, that motto also appeared in a school not far from here, Bordentown Military Academy. I remember running into it twice in my academic career, there and later at college. I can't give you the full Latin, I'm sorry. There are others who will have to supply the exact text. But the essence of it was that there was a *qui sciret* in it, an *exprimit,* and a *nesciret* and literally translated it runs: "He who knows and cannot express what he knows is as he who knows not." That is a very literal, but I think almost the best, translation of that Latin motto.

I've seen, on so many occasions, a decision on a very important issue made as the result of some clear, simple statement by a man around a conference table. I've seen clarity of expression by a less brilliant individual win the day so many more times, it seems to me, than the confused statement of a more brilliant one that I urge you earnestly to cultivate the art of good expression if you hope to have your views prevail at critical times.

It's interesting, also, and I'll come back to Lawton Collins for just a minute, that thirty days before the D Day at Normandy I was in an auditorium of a school known as St. Paul's School in London. It happened to be the very school that Field Marshal Montgomery of England had attended as a boy. I don't know whether it was a coincidence or not—I'm sure that it must have been but, perhaps, knowing Montgomery, he might have arranged it himself— that that should be his headquarters before the invasion.

In this auditorium there was set up, for a period of two days, a complete exposition of how the attack across the Normandy beaches was to move. Each corps commander, each division commander, and each army commander was compelled to stand on a great platform very much like this, only it was larger, leading up to an organ loft. The platform was a great map—a relief map on which men could walk back and forth but on such a slant that all in the audience could see the map.

All the mighty of England were there. It took all the king's horses and all the king's men to get into the secret session, but when you were once up there, they unfolded from the beginning to the end the entire story of the attack. Churchill spoke; Montgomery spoke; Bradley spoke; and so on it went. They finally got down to corps commanders, and this man Lawton Collins got up again, and he spoke. And his exposition was so clear and so graphic that it stirred people in their chairs. I happened to be sitting just behind Mr. Churchill and Mr. Eden. Churchill turned around to me and said, "Who was that man? That was the finest exposition of the whole day."

Well, it was the same fellow who had given the talk at Fort Knox to which General Marshall had listened many years before and which was probably as much responsible as any other one thing for Lawton Collins being where he was on that day in London. Now there's a real plug for the English Department!

Who are these unknown figures who suddenly appear wielding tremendous authority? Where do they come from? They are no group of geniuses fortuitously provided by Providence to meet historical emergencies. Nor are they great inspirational leaders. Men like Mr. Roosevelt and

Mr. Churchill are the rare dispensers of inspiration. Such figures have the vision splendid, but others have to "implement" the vision. And it's that group—the common ordinary everyday garden variety of talent and character— which carried on the pace of the war.

It's not unreasonable to imagine that if these men had singly been trained for the particular tasks they performed they would not have been equal to the emergency. To prepare for all of the eventualities that arose they would have had to have gathered so much general information and thus have been so saddled with the weight of it that their powers of decision would have been impaired. The architects of victory were, by and large, ordinary people drawn from routine peaceful occupations, men who had a good general intellectual background, with fundamental character and the habit of applying themselves fully to their tasks.

Now, the onset of the emergencies and the pressure of critical decisions did not stop, unfortunately, with the end of the war. The United States and the entire world are faced now and will be faced in the years to come with issues even more far reaching in their implications than those we faced during the war. Such developments as the release of atomic energy, the fundamental transformation in the international balance of power, the growth of communism backed by the might of the Soviet Union, the tide of nationalism and political unrest in Asia, Africa, Latin America, and the urge toward closer economic and political integration in the Western world; all these constitute tests, or if you will examinations, for us to pass or fail, as well as for those who follow us.

In this time of reassessment, of reorganization, of revolution in the broadest sense of the term, it is impossible to blueprint the pattern of the future, or to define an exact course of action, just as it was impossible for Eisenhower to be sure of the weather on that morning in June, 1944. All that we can do is establish our basic principles, the essential values we believe in, and chart a general course for the immediate future. But we must expect certain emergencies that require quick judgments, changes of plan, and just as during the war, the success or failure of our endeavors will depend on the men who make the key decisions.

The formulation of the Marshall Plan is an example of the type of critical decision that may determine the course of events for many years. I happen to believe that the program is fundamentally sound and truly constructive, but neither I, nor anyone else, can say with assurance that it will succeed. During the past few months I've seen some very cogent memoranda and statistical presentations that purport to prove that the recovery program cannot accomplish its purpose. And, on the other hand, I've seen equally convincing proofs that it can and that it will.

These things cannot be demonstrated statistically. The human element is too important. Such matters as the expansion of productive investment, the reopening of channels of trade with individual countries, and, of course, national frontiers, the productivity of the labor force are only determined by tangible economic factors. But the decisive influences are very largely psychological and individual in character, and they depend upon public confidence.

Today, I believe that in Europe the problem isn't by any means solely a problem of rebuilding physical capacity.

The plants are there in very large measure, the machine tools are there, the lathes are there. It's amazing how much has been done since the war to rebuild the productive capacity of Europe. It's amazing how much was not destroyed. Although we see pictures everywhere of the destruction of Europe, I think anyone who was in Europe in 1945, and who again visited Europe in 1948, would be as much impressed with the restoration and rehabilitation of the country as he would be by the still existing ruins. The thing that Europe lacks today, more than any other one thing, is confidence. It is the sinews of trade and the nervous system of trade that constitute the great lack, the things that make it easy for people to cross borders, the existence of currencies in which people have faith, the sort of thing that makes the farmer send his product to market. It is the restoration of that type of product, I think, much more than bricks and mortar that Europe is dependent on today. And those are elements that involve imponderables and that profoundly depend on human values of the nature of which I speak.

When we look back upon the great mistakes in human judgment that the Nazis made, I think this point is emphasized. They disastrously underestimated the capacity and the will, for example, of the British people to resist, as well as the strength and the determination of the people of the United States to produce and to fight. And more recently the antidemocratic propagandists have been able, without much difficulty, to delude themselves that our efforts of postwar construction must inevitably fail and that economic liberalism is foredoomed to collapse.

When I read of these prophecies of disaster, I remember our situation in 1933 when the national income of the

United States had fallen to about thirty billion dollars a year, and we had millions of unemployed workers. It was asserted at that time, with the support of elaborate statistical curves and graphs, that the expansion of our economy had come to an end. We were getting old as a nation, we were told, and we couldn't develop ourselves as we had in our youth. In our declining years we must be resigned to progressive hardening of the joints and arteries of our economy and to the gradual approach of national senility.

Today, fifteen years later, we have over sixty million people employed on our farms and our factories and in our trade. Our national income has risen to over two hundred billions a year, and our exports make the difference between economic revival and collapse, even between life and death, for hundreds of millions of people living abroad. It turned out that the United States was not so decrepit as had been assumed. I am convinced that we can continue this healthy growth for a good many years to come if we have the necessary spirit and leadership. The same hopeful prospect, with a similar qualification, seems to me to exist for international recovery.

So far I've emphasized the impossibility in any great human undertaking of surveying all the factors involved so as to arrive at a mathematically sure decision with fully predictable consequences. And this is certainly true of a period with such widespread ferment as we have now. Our future security and welfare depend upon our having in key positions men who are not hobbled by overrigid habits of thought, whose initiative has not been killed by too oppressive authority, and who are not tired out from past frustrations and compromises. It is not possible to develop such leaders overnight when the emergency strikes.

They have to be drawn from the reservoirs of society as a whole. And one of the springs of that reservoir is such places as schools of this type. One of our basic objectives must be to perfect and maintain the type of social and educational systems that will best preserve these springs.

Political philosophers in ancient times gave a good deal of thought to how you develop leaders. Plato proposed, with his philosopher king, that they should be educated from infancy to fit them for absolute rule. The Nazis had somewhat the same idea, with a different emphasis, on the leadership principle. They were to establish elite schools of Nazi youth trained only to command. But to my mind the system that is developed in our society, and of which this school is an outstanding example, is fundamentally wiser and more likely to succeed. We pin our faith on the principle of individual responsibility. Our aim is to encourage initiative at all levels of social activity, with authority and responsibility following on the basis of demonstrated merit.

Napoleon explained the success of the French armies against the mercenaries and the caste-ridden forces of his enemies by saying that each man had a baton in his knapsack. Every man, however obscure his origins, had the opportunity to rise as far as his individual capacity allowed. And the tremendous response of the French troops to this challenge carried them to the very ends of Europe. And the same principle must apply today.

In a time of social transition and confusion the tight disciplines of totalitarian forces seem to give them great advantage. But I'm quite confident that such an advantage is temporary, that the totalitarian system is eventually self-defeating. The great issues of our time are too complicated to be met successfully by repeating established dogma or by transmitting orders down through a rigid hierarchy.

There are some who believe that democracy is too decadent, too divided, too indecisive, ever to compete successfully with the newer totalitarian religions. I simply do not believe it. More than anything else we need to reaffirm the ideals and the purposes that we sometimes have taken too much for granted, for it is in its democratic faith as well as in its physical power that the strength of America lies.

There are so many opportunities left in the United States with the development of atomic energy as only one example that we never need to think that this country has lost its pioneer opportunities. And if you don't find those opportunities in this country, you can find them at hand all over the world. I've just come from South America where the expanses are so tremendous that they stagger your imagination as you fly over them. There is no lack of opportunity.

I am reminded, as I was at the beginning, of a story—another story—of Mr. Churchill's, which I think is an inspiring one. I remember he spoke one of his greatest speeches at a time when things looked very black indeed, and he talked about the opportunities that were still ahead for the British Empire, even at that point. If they were before the British Empire then, how much more truly are they before the United States at this point! He ended up his great speech by saying, "Dread naught, dread naught, and all will be well." I give you that thought for your future.

Cord Meyer, Jr.

SINCE THE BEST possible introduction to this essay is embodied in the one that follows, it would be an impertinence for me to add more here. What Meyer has to say should be read in conjunction with the thoughts and point of view of Norman Cousins. The introduction I refer to appears in Cousins's essay, pages 35-48.

T. H. J.

THE NEW ENVIRONMENT

by Cord Meyer, Jr.

I'D LIKE TO begin by thinking about the new environment in which we find ourselves, an environment that I can take for granted you know a great deal about. I speak particularly of the weapons that have been developed in the last few years, because they have completely changed the kind of a world we must now inhabit. I'd like to begin with the atomic bomb.

Perhaps you do not know that the bomb that was used at Hiroshima is a very primitive device even now and that we have developed much more effective ones, and that bombs ten to a hundred times as effective are to be expected in the near future. Perhaps you did not know that the radioactive effects of the atomic bomb, and the radioactive cloud that is now available, may have hereditary effects and that if atomic bombs were used in a war not only would millions be killed but those who survived would risk having their children and children's children born deformed and mentally deficient. These facts should be kept in mind. Then there are the biological weapons of which you have probably read. The fact is that we, in the United States, now have available seventeen various diseases that we can spread among an enemy population and that we have the means of delivering these weapons in the form of long-range bombers and rockets, which are in process of development. In none of these weapons can America have a lasting monopoly. Biological weapons, germs, are easily developed as the official Merck report pointed out; they could be made, as one biologist remarked, in a beer vat. They can be made in quantity, and they do not demand a large industrial capacity. Probably, at the present time, a number of countries are armed with them, including ourselves. The atomic bomb, as you know, can be made by any highly industrialized nation. The scientific knowledge is widespread and cannot be kept secret. Within two to six years, many scientists are convinced, Russia and a number of other countries will be armed with atomic bombs. The monopoly cannot be kept. All other countries have long-range bombers. Other countries are in the process of developing rockets. These are the facts of life. There is no defense against these weapons. For protection against an attack launched with such weapons as these, a defense would have to be one hundred per cent effective; it would have to be capable of knocking down all the attacking planes and rockets. Because if one plane, armed with atomic bombs, gets through on a city that is sufficient.

Now, no such hundred-per-cent effective defense against aircraft and rockets is remotely conceivable. Therefore we can say with assurance that there *is* no defense that means anything, that can offer any protection to us. The United States is today, then, capable of delivering an attack against any other nation in the Northern Hemisphere and in that attack—in the first moments of it—annihilating its urban civilization—the people who live in its cities and the industries of those cities. If not today, in the immediate future, other countries will be capable of doing the same thing to us. This is the reality we have to face. This fact defines the environment that, for better or worse, we must now inhabit.

Faced with this new power to destroy that we have developed through our ingenuity, the American people seem to be faced with three basic alternatives. The first alternative is this: we can continue to seek national security by remaining the strongest military power in the world. If we can't protect the country when we are actually attacked, we can attempt to prevent any country from launching an attack against us merely by the obvious size and efficiency of our preparations for a counteroffensive. In other words, we can attempt to terrify the rest of the world into peace merely by the extreme measures of preparedness we've taken. We can be prepared to strike back after losing our major cities, our industries, and one third of our people. This is the policy of peace through intimidation, of preparing for the retaliatory war. This is the policy toward which our present bipartisan foreign policy is now moving. I have left out the obvious, that if we adopt this policy of attempting to protect ourselves by the very size of our preparations for a counteroffensive other countries will do likewise. Every increase in our armed power will provoke a corresponding increase in the power of others, and the nations of the world will become committed to an armament race, to a competition for arms, strategic bases, war matériel, and allies stretching over the entire world. Now, in this competition, which has already begun, we have only one possible competitor, and that country is the Soviet Union. Only the United States and Russia survived World War II with sufficient strength to fight again. It is not so much ideological differences or differences between economic systems that have caused the struggle between the United States and Russia. On the contrary, they are natural rivals because of the size of their territory, population, and industrial potential. They are, each of them, the only threat to the security of the other, because they are the only two countries in the world now capable of hoping for victory in another war.

Let us suppose that this armament race continues. Let's suppose we accept this first alternative and prepare ourselves for the retaliatory war. What will be necessary in this country? We can't attempt to win the armament race simply by building more atomic bombs, rockets, and bombers than our possible opponent. That country which is capable of protecting from atomic attack its vital industry and vital sections of its population by subterranean dispersal will enjoy the decisive advantage in any future war. In other words, the vast war potential of our industrial structure will be wiped out in the first moment of another war unless we disperse and decentralize. City dwellers must be gotten out of the city and evacuated into the country areas if we are to protect them. This program of dispersal and decentralization is an absolute necessity in any modern program of preparedness.

Now it must be clear that such a dispersal program is going to involve tremendous changes in the political and economic structure of our country. In the first place, such a program might cost well over three hundred billion dollars. That's one estimate. In order to enforce decentralization, to get the industries out of the city, we would have to centralize political power in this country. It could only be done through authoritarian rule from the top down. The cost of such a program, three hundred billion, would involve a very steep decline in our living standards. Antisabotage and antiespionage precautions would restrict and finally eliminate our civil liberties. The search for allies would lead us into supporting any regime, no matter how corrupt and tyrannical, so long as it opposed our enemies. Finally, when these measures of preparedness had been taken and we had turned our country into a vast military machine, poised for instantaneous retaliation, then preparedness would be complete, and life of the individual citizen of this country would be one prolonged agony of oppression and suspense. Totalitarianism in the United States, total control of the life of the individual by the government, a police-state military camp, is the price of preparedness in a world consisting of a number of nations armed with modern weapons. That we would see.

Now, even if the American people submit themselves to these sacrifices, will they gain peace thereby? I don't think so. What is already being created is a chain reaction of mutual fear and suspicion. Each preparedness measure that we take looks to Russia like preparedness for an aggressive war. We, in turn, suspect that they're intending to commit aggression. And so the fires of mutual suspicion are fed. And sooner or later one nation or the other will strike first in fear that if it waits the other country will employ the advantage of the initiative. You can't build peace on mutual terror. The end result of the armament race that has begun will be war, and we will delude ourselves if we think that peace can be built on competitive armaments.

In such a war, fought with these weapons, the cities of the earth would be eradicated, and the victor would inherit a wasteland of ruins, among which the survivors would wander in absolute desolation. We would destroy the structure and fabric of what we like to call civilization. And a new dark age, lasting for how many years I do not know, would begin.

Faced with this alternative, realizing the difficulties and dangers of a prolonged armament race, there are many in this country now who think of a second alternative, and that alternative is preventive war. There are many who are saying, "Let us fight now. Let us attack Russia now while we have atomic bombs and they do not." This is the argument presented by James Burnham recently in *Life* magazine and in his book, the argument you hear ever more often throughout the country, and because it is growing more popular, I'd like to take a moment to do what I can to refute it.

You must realize that morally preventive war is a polite name for aggression. The mere suspicion that our victim was planning to attack at some future, indefinite date would not mitigate our guilt or justify our initial attack. Preventive war is the crime for which we hung the Nazi leaders at Nuremberg, and if we intend to wage it, we had better pay our apologies to Hitler, Himmler, and Goering. Practically, preventive war is not as easy as it has been made to appear by its supporters. It would not end with the eradication of Moscow and Leningrad. The initial atomic attack of the United States against Russia would provoke an immediate sweep of the Russian infantry through Western Europe, into the Middle East, and into China. We would become involved in a prolonged continental campaign involving millions of casualties. Russia, being probably already armed with biological weapons, would feel justified in using those weapons against us to spread incurable epidemics among our people if we attacked first with atomic bombs.

Suppose we finally won this war. That is, after Europe had been completely ruined and devastated in the process. What would we have then? We would immediately have to establish over the entire face of the earth a ruthless tyranny to prevent those seeking revenge, our victims, from ever constructing the weapons that we used, to use against us. This tyranny would be unstable. Civil war would reign throughout, and eventually it would collapse ignominiously from internal revolt, dissension, and revenge. This is the American century that the preventive war will lead to. Must despair then have the last word? I don't think so. There is a third alternative, and that is to find, with the Soviet Union and the other nations, a cooperative solution of the security problem. Good-will gestures of unilateral disarmament are meaningless, dangerous, and futile. While other nations are free to prepare for war, we must also. But we must offer to join with other countries in strengthening the United Nations into a reliable and effective system of international security.

Now, what has been done in that direction already? Well, the United States government has offered the Baruch Plan, and many think that in offering the Baruch Plan we have done all within our power to end the arms race and to bring peace. But let's take a closer look at the Baruch Plan. Is it a realistic plan that will work? I think that it was offered in genuine sincerity and seriousness, but I think if we look at it closely we'll see that there are fatal defects.

As you know, the Baruch Plan proposed that the United States would give up its atomic bombs on condition that all other countries agreed to a system of international control and inspection and on condition that the veto power be given up in so far as it applies to enforcement action. Well now, one of the defects of the Baruch Plan is the fact that it dealt only with atomic bombs. Apparently the idea was that we were going first to control atomic bombs and then we'd go on to other weapons. But this means, in effect, that we would try to control atomic weapons while the competition continued among all countries for all other types of weapons: biological, bombers, rockets, mechanized divisions, warships, and the like. Now, is this conceivable? Would the United States Senate agree to it? Would the United States Senate agree to giving up our atomic bombs while the Red Army remained mobilized and while we had no assurance that they were not producing biological weapons? That's one defect, it seems to me. Security is indivisible and cannot be achieved by banning one particular type of weapon. You're not going to stop the next war by drafting Marquis of Queensberry rules that will be ignored the minute the conflict occurs. I hope in the question period we can go deeper into the Baruch Plan, and some of the other defects can be made clear, because it is important that we realize that the Baruch Plan is not the last and final offer we must make. The Baruch Plan is not enough. We must go beyond it if we are to do all that we can to avoid another conflict.

Now, if we seriously intend to have peace, if we intend to avoid the kind of war that would be fought with the weapons now available, we must settle for nothing less than a U.N. that is strong enough to prevent all war between nations and to prevent and prohibit preparations for war. These seem to me to be the basic amendments, changes, necessary in the structure of the U.N.

First, the U.N. must be given the power to administer laws binding on individuals and to which they owe their first duty. In other words, no national government can have the right to override these basic world laws. And this lawmaking authority of the U.N. must be limited only to those matters essential to security. What are they? I think there are three of them. One, the U.N. must have the power to prohibit the manufacture, ownership, or use of the major weapons of warfare, not just atomic bombs and biological weapons but all the major weapons of warfare. Nations must be substantially disarmed. Secondly, the U.N. must have the power to prohibit acts of aggression and the use of force in the settlement of international disputes. Thirdly, it must regulate and control the peaceful development of atomic power. Now the U.N. must not have only this power. It must have the power to arrest and try in world courts, with compulsory jurisdiction, individuals who violate the world security code. What we have to have is a legal procedure under which we can hold a Nuremburg trial before twenty million people have been killed instead of after. We want to have a system that can stop the would-be aggressor before he has had an opportunity to launch his country into war. And we must have an inspection system. The U.N. must have the power to conduct an international system of inspection, these inspectors having free access into all countries, and they must conduct a continuous search for all attempts to produce illegal arms. And this is the most important element. We must have a world police force. The U.N. must have the power to recruit—that's on a volunteer basis

—individuals from each nation into a police force that will owe exclusive allegiance to the U.N. It will be organized on an international basis. It will be strategically distributed throughout the world and will be armed with the most effective modern weapons. Until the nations, the United States, Russia, and the rest, are willing to give to the U.N. itself the preponderant military power to keep the peace, they will be condemned to compete in a futile effort to surpass each other. Now, obviously these increases of authority in the U.N. will involve some change in its internal structure. The Security Council must be made into an executive cabinet responsible to the Assembly for the execution of these laws. And once the Security Code has been accepted as essential to the common safety of all nations, then, naturally, no nations can retain the right to veto enforcement action of those laws.

Now, you can call this world government if you want to, but it's government on the federal principle. The nations would be free to conduct their domestic affairs as they saw fit. National governments would be giving up only the right and means of internal annihilation, only the right and means of waging war, and that is a right they must give up if they intend to survive in this new environment.

In this problem the United States has the initiative. We manufactured, produced, and used atomic bombs. We are the most powerful country today, militarily speaking, and unless we take the initiative, no one else will. With power goes responsibility. Once we realize and understand that no amount of money, arms, or men can delay war for long or protect this country when war comes, it would appear that we have a right and a duty to demand of our government that it propose such measures as are essential for our protection.

Now, other countries. What about them? Well, England is already committed to this policy in the person of Foreign Secretary Bevin, who has reiterated and repeated again and again that he is ready to make these sacrifices of sovereignty. The responsible leaders of many other countries have already indicated that they are ready to do this. So it is the United States and Russia that are the stumbling blocks. Suppose the United States makes the offer. What about Russia? Will she accept? I do not think we can tell that until we make the offer. I, personally, believe that if the offer is made there is a good chance that Russia will accept, because a continued arms race ending in a suicidal and mutually destructive conflict is no more to the advantage of the Kremlin than it is to our interest. And in the hard fact that another conflict would be suicidal for them as for us lies the best hope, and the real reason, for thinking that Russia will accept. At least we know this: that there is no way of finding out whether Russian war preparations are aggressive or defensive in purpose, except to make this offer.

Churchill in a recent speech said that we have five years to set up this government I am now defining to you. Five years. I don't think that he was pessimistic. I think that he may have been optimistic, because we do not have much time. Politically, every day that goes past sees a growth of mutual suspicion as both countries amass the means of annihilating each other. Soon, propaganda and preparedness will have driven national leaders in both countries past all hope of turning back. I don't think that a shooting war is imminent, but I do think that we may soon pass the point when both countries will have adopted policies that will eventually make war inevitable. Before that critical point is passed, we must act.

In conclusion, what can we do in this limited period of grace that remains to us? Individually, as members of the human race, we can make sure that we are well informed, that we know what is going on and how our fate is involved with what is going on, that we know the facts, that we use our brains and think with our brains and not with slogans and propaganda. Collectively, once you have thought the problem through, you as students can act together, through an organization known as the Student Division of the United World Federalists. You can act together to inform those other students around you on what the facts are, to inform your family, parents, your home and community, in a program of mass education and information. And this is a great deal and it can be done, and it must be done soon.

There are many people who resign themselves to the future. People who say there is nothing they can do about it, that men have always fought and they will continue to fight. Well, I don't think that that resignation is justified or necessary. It seems to me that when the American people and the rest of the people of the world understand that their choice is really between some measure of world government, or world destruction—they will choose to live.

Norman Cousins

As EDITOR SINCE 1942 of the *Saturday Review of Literature,* Norman Cousins has been influencing public opinion through his policy and editorials quite beyond the circulation of the journal itself. He was one of the reporters present at Bikini, and here is an eyewitness account of the atom-bomb explosion.

He is in the tradition of those who recognize a moral obligation to be intelligent. "One thousand years of human history were eclipsed in that brief fraction of a second during which the atomic bomb exploded over Hiroshima." The challenge of this new era, the need for world government, is the subject of his essay.

T. H. J.

DON'T RESIGN FROM THE HUMAN RACE

by *Norman Cousins*

OUR YEARS AGO, hostility and division within the UN were regarded as a luxury. I wonder whether they are any less a luxury today than they were four years ago. You know, you have only to take the rate of disintegration, the rate of unraveling in the world in the last one year and project it against the next year to see where you come out. How much longer can this continue before you have a saturation of tension? I say this quite seriously. I'm not attempting to be melodramatic; I'm not attempting to exploit fear. Some months ago I spoke on a similar theme. Afterward someone got up and said, "Why, you're just a fear monger. You're trying to throw terror into our hearts." It didn't occur to me that that was what I was doing, because this is a valid question: What do you do when a man's house is on fire? Do you feel that perhaps if you inform him of the fact he might run into the fire? Do you withhold the information because of the possibility that he might not do anything about it or will react adversely? Of course, he might not call the fire department. I don't know. But the only question to answer is this: How do you *know* that the house *is* on fire? Again, I ask you merely to project the rate of disintegration of the last year against the next year to see where you come out. Is there in the world today, anything,

35

any agency, with adequate authority to keep the peace?

What about the United Nations? Well, four years ago in San Francisco there was a great and valid hope. And that hope was expressed in the Preamble to the Charter of the United Nations, to wit: "We, the people of the United Nations, determine to prevent the scourge of war, to hereby...," etc. But when it came time to set it up inside the UN—the actual machinery which could keep the peace —the nations of the world held back. We live in a time and in a world where you can get from Lawrenceville, New Jersey, to Chungking, China, in less time than it took to get from Princeton to Philadelphia one hundred and sixty years ago. We live in a world and in a time when, starting at Lawrenceville, you can fly around the world twice in the time it took to get from Lawrenceville to Washington one hundred and sixty years ago. We live in a world where all nations and all peoples have better access to each other for purposes of association—or destruction.

I was unfortunate enough to see what happened when the atomic bomb went off three years ago. I say "unfortunate enough" because I perhaps might have slept better since that time if I hadn't seen it. We were stationed on the third deck of the U.S.S. *Appalachian,* below the communication ship. And behind us was a naval officer who was counting off the minutes before zero. He alone knew the precise second at which the atomic bomb would be released from the plane over the target. At ten minutes before dawn the naval officer announced that the plane had reached its assigned height, had completed its second test run over target, and was now bearing down for the live run. At eight minutes before zero the ship's motors stopped. At six minutes before zero we put on our goggles. They're practically opaque, and only by turning around and looking at the sun did you know that these were actually goggles and not actually some joke that a fellow correspondent was playing on you. At four minutes before zero you became conscious of the fact that the intervals were much longer than they were at the start, that, for example, it was much longer between six minutes and four minutes than it had been between eight minutes and six minutes. At two minutes before zero you began thinking about two rather interesting things. At four minutes before zero I thought it might be nice to see the family again. At two minutes before zero I happened to see a face before me in my mind, that of Harold Urey, the Nobel Prize physicist, the founder of the principle of gaseous diffusion, one of the three chief thinkers in the development of atomic energy for military purposes.

I thought of Urey because I remembered how he had looked just one month before I left Bikini. He had aged thirty years in just a few years since I had seen him before the war, thirty years in just a few years. I know I spoke to his friends about it. They said that Urey aged those thirty years, not during the time he worked on the atomic-bomb project but aged those thirty years in the one year since the end of the war. And then when you asked Urey about it, he told you quite frankly that what had happened in one year was to him much more taxing than anything that had happened during those years he had worked on the atomic-energy project.

Here's what he said: "While I worked on the Manhattan District Project the only thought that sustained me was the fact that I was absolutely certain that we could build this planet-shattering weapon and the control at the end of the war. That helped me to retain my sanity. But here," he said, "here it is one year after, and the world still does not have atomic control."

You thought of that. You thought of the fact, for example, that Dr. Oppenheimer, in testimony before the Senate committee on atomic energy, had said that if there should be an atomic war the casualties in the United States would be thirty million in the first waves upon attack. Dr. Oppenheimer said that every city with one hundred thousand population and over could be destroyed. And while I was thinking of these things, the naval officer behind me said, very faintly, "Bomb away."

For fifty-seven seconds the bomb fell before it exploded. I assure you it easily seemed more like fifty-seven years. I'm not fifty-seven years old, but I tell you truthfully that I think I lived more during those fifty-seven seconds than I did in all the years leading up to it. It's hard to explain.

What happened was that you were conscious of nothing. Time and space were exploded in a vacuum. You knew that you could lift off your goggles and look at the waves and the waves would be motionless. And suddenly you could look at the men beside you. They'd be like statues, as indeed they were. And still the bomb fell. I suppose that when the enemy's attacking every second is an eternity. I've often thought of those fifty-seven seconds, thought of that experience particularly when people say that if you will allow just a year or two to set up the regime of daily peace, then we can escape somewhere. Escape may mean buying a season ticket to see the Dodgers or going out to the Fiji Islands. You can take your choice.

I thought of those fifty-seven seconds because I thought

of them as not time but decision. What you decide to do within the time you have. It makes no difference whether that time happens to be ten years or one year or two months. The main thing is that you make up your mind as to what you are going to do. Just how long fifty-seven seconds can be!

The very thought of the explosion! It was rich, round, red, and large, and you ripped off your goggles, and there, far off on the horizon was a small, fat clot of black smoke sitting very comfortably on the sea. But then it rises from it very quickly as though it had been concealed beneath the surface of the sea—a cylindrical shaft, a long white column—twisting as it rose, spiraling, moving with the wind, flecked with pinks and blues and reds, and rising very fast and then flattening out at the top into the very familiar symbol of the mushroom. When you looked at it with horrified fascination, it was not because it was a horrifying spectacle. It wasn't. You looked at it with horror because you realized that what you were seeing was the standardization of catastrophe, the fact that this was very familiar to millions of people all over the world, that the world had now known four atomic bombs, with a new atomic bomb to come within a few weeks, and God knows how many atomic bombs after that.

I don't think that the reporters on board the deck of the *Appalachian* were in a good position then to report back on the tragedy concerning what was happening on Bikini, because we didn't know. We had only the report of an overhead plane to go by, and yet we had the assignment to broadcast. They put a microphone in front of you, and you spoke perhaps for ten minutes on something that happened in a flash. You knew nothing about what was happening in the lagoon. The report from the plane over-head said that the *Nevada* was afloat, that all the ships were afloat, and so you reported that over the air, and meanwhile the reporters jumped to their typewriters to relay the information that the fleet was intact. And yet it was not until three days later that we actually knew what was happening in the Bikini lagoon.

We couldn't go into the lagoon for three days because of radioactivity. The ships were still hot; the water was still hot. After three days we cruised into the lagoon, for-tified with Geiger counters—those black little boxes that determine the amount of radioactivity in the air—and we cruised up within about three hundred yards of the center of the target array, the U.S.S. *Nevada*. There the fantail looked as though it had been twisted by some giant. Then we looked off to the left and saw the *Salt Lake City,* the main mast cut in half, and a Japanese battleship listing badly, about to sink. The Japanese cruiser, *Nagato,* had by this time a twenty-degree list, and yet that wasn't the real damage because we discovered by a process of tri-angulation that the bomb had missed its target by half a **mile.**

Despite this fact the damage was indescribable. Take for example the case of the aircraft carrier *Independence.* Here you had once proud walls of steel rising up eighty feet from the sea. It seemed as though the same giant fingers had thrust through that steel wall, had taken six decks and crumpled them in a meaningless jumble of shredded steel and tin. The ship was completely gutted. The question is: How is it that only six ships were sunk? Well, the fact of the matter is that the damage was topside. But the important thing to remember about Bikini is not the blast, not the heat, but that those ships today are still radioactive and still unsafe.

And why do I bring this out? Largely because a revolution has happened in the last few years. One thousand years of human history were eclipsed in that brief fraction of a second during which the atomic bomb exploded over Hiroshima presenting a challenge to all of us. And when I say "all of us," I mean, all of us. It chalked out one thousand years in our thinking.

To catch up I'd like to tell you about one man who did catch up. His name is Cord Meyer. He is a Marine veteran. Several years ago on Guadalcanal he was alone in a foxhole, and he was thinking about his brother who, two weeks before that, had been killed on Iwo Jima. Enemy shells began coming over. Then, as he wrote about it, a giant club rose up and hit him in the face, and there was a blinding light for a second, and after awhile he put his hand to his face and felt for his eye. It was no longer there. And that night while he lay in that foxhole waiting for medical attention—not knowing whether he was going to live, not knowing whether he would ever see again—he began to think about many things, and he knew that a world that would permit the continuance of this order of war would inevitably destroy itself.

Now, when Cord Meyer came back it was logical and inevitable, I think, that a boy with this inspirational quality should be called upon by such men as Chief Justice Douglas, by such men as Thomas Finletter, the chairman of the President's air-policy commission, by such authors as Carl van Doren, to lead the world-government movement inside the United States. He is twenty-eight years old. And people tell him that world government today is impossible. And he laughs at it—laughs to himself—because, you see, these men on Guadalcanal were asked to *do* the impossible and they did it.

He knows, for example, of one mission at the beginning of the war in which the Japanese were only one and a half days from Midway. They had a flotilla of forty ships bearing down on Midway. This was the crucial point of the war, not long after Pearl Harbor. If the Japanese had been able to seize Midway, they might have been able to move on to Honolulu, to Hawaii, and perhaps from there to the West Coast. We had nothing to stop them. Our battleships and aircraft carriers were in the mud of Pearl Harbor. There was nothing on the West Coast of the United States. The only thing we had that could possibly stop that flotilla from bearing down on Midway was the assembly line of Willow Run: planes that hadn't even been tested.

Forty planes were ripped off that assembly line and flown for the first time by men who had no time to adjust themselves to new ships. They were flown in formations and went out on their first operation, and stopped the Japanese fleet at Midway! Any military man who knew that the Japanese were only a day and a half away from Midway would have said the odds against us were a hundred to one. A hundred to one against us. And yet, that's the challenge of life.

And Meyer knows that our generation has had to do the impossible, that we've done it before and can do it again. And yet there is no defense against atomic attack. You can't beat the atom bomb by war. There's only one defense, and that defense is peace.

And that is why Cord Meyer and hundreds of thousands of people around the country, especially in the schools and the colleges, are now joining in a crusade to establish a world government, before it is too late, in the attempt to give the United Nations the authority it now needs to keep the peace. At San Francisco, when it came time actually to set up the UN, the large nations all held back. Each nation thought that it could look out for its interests only through unilateralism. The United States proposed the veto at San Francisco.

Security in the world today means expansion, because the world outside of Russia and the United States is a power vacuum and each side is attempting to fill it lest it be filled by the other. Let's keep this in mind: In all of recorded history the world has been at peace for only three hundred years. Indeed, some anthropologists will tell you that war is actually part of the instinct of man, and they point out that only two species on this planet practice the art of organized war against their own kind: men and ants. But so far as we know, the ants have not yet discovered atomic energy, so there's little danger that they will run out of ants to fight wars with.

Man's problem is somewhat more complicated. He has reached the point in his development where he has exhausted his margin for error, where every move now must be the right one, where he can no longer afford the final mistake of war. And yet, war as such is not the ultimate. If you are going to eliminate war only to have injustice, then we might just as well fight. Peace can be had at too high a price if the cost of peace is slavery, as it would have been—as it might yet be—and so peace by itself means nothing. Peace, as Mr. Whitehead pointed out, can be anesthesia. The important thing is to have peace through justice.

43

Now what is it that we want? We'd like to be sure that we can have peace in the United States, and you can have peace only by having control of all weapons adapted to mass destruction. You know that we can't have control without power, but you know, too, that power can become brutal. So you want to make sure that power is subject to law.

How do you get law? The law is the product of government, so you level a direct line for a desire for security to the least of government which alone can assure that security. Is it one thousand years away? Is it too idealistic, too difficult? The only thing greater than the difficulty in getting world government is the danger of not getting it. We in the United States are not without experience in the business of erecting laws. One hundred and sixty years ago we were confronted with many differences among the American nations, differences so acute that Noah Webster, the lexicographer, who traveled up and down the land, wrote about his difficulties. He said, "What's more, my currency would shrink ten percent just in the act of crossing a state line. . . . I could hardly make myself understood. The differences in languages! in customs! in religions! And now in our life all these things make it extremely difficult for a traveler. . . . I don't think it will ever be possible to accommodate all these nations within the design of a single government."

And yet, at Philadelphia, it was precisely because these differences threatened to erupt in war that it became necessary to bring the American nations together.

I heard Dr. Nicholas Murray Butler at Columbia say that not one student out of ten thousand properly understood the meaning of American history as it concerned the correct relationship between the War for Independence and the Constitution. "Most of us," he said, "study our history books very carefully. We come away with a confused impression as though the American Revolution and the Constitution are part of the same historical package." Actually, as he pointed out, there is a cause-and-effect relationship between the War for Independence and the Articles of Confederation. It was the fact that these states were virtually at the brink of war that made it necessary for them to come together, not despite the differences, but because of the differences. If those differences had been permitted to continue, the United States would have had anarchy.

Now, what is it that we'd like to see the United Nations have? Even if we managed to abolish the veto, nations could still inflict their will on the majority by walking out, as Germany, Italy, and Japan did in the old League. So make sure when you get rid of the veto that you have a system of compulsory jurisdiction backed by preponderant force. Thus any decision you make must have the force of law behind it.

Take the assembly within the United Nations. The assembly at San Francisco was set up on a one-nation, one-veto method of representation. Nicaragua and Honduras and Costa Rica, let us say, with a population of four or five million, could outvote the United States and Great Britain combined. The large nations might never agree to giving any essential powers to the assembly. What then about the Security Council, which was designed to keep the peace? There you have exactly the opposite: organized statism. And so the time has now come to make fundamental changes within the construction of the United

Nations. The United Nations must have access to the individual and the authority of the individual only in those various very specific matters clearly related to world security.

Let me give you an example as to how this might work. Let us suppose that in Lawrenceville some night someone were to break into your room and burglarize it. You would call on the local police because that act of burglary constitutes a direct threat to anyone in the community itself. We have the local police for that purpose. Or suppose you happen to be speeding in a car. You'd find that the State Police could pick you up for that crime and that crime alone. Again we see the area of a common security determines the area of jurisdiction. Suppose that you devise a rather questionable hobby known as making your own money. The Federal government, I assure you, before very long will slice through the state and the city and get you for that crime and that crime alone, because everyone in the United States is endangered by counterfeit money. So there again we see the principle that the area of a common security determines the extent of the jurisdiction.

On the world scale, how about crimes committed by individuals? It is clear that anyone anywhere who is engaged in the manufacture of proscribed weapons constitutes a threat to the lives of all the people in the world, and no nation must be allowed to shield him. That would be an act against the world community, and the UN must have the authority to reach down and get the individuals, because the heart of law is access to the individual.

All these three steps, compulsory jurisdiction, preponderance of force, access to the individual, may seem to be a thousand miles away. I can only say that it is unfortunate

46

for the human race that we need it today. I can only say that if ten per cent of us are not ready for it, then the human race is ready for anything that it really needs, because I don't propose to resign from the human race. The time has come for the United States, finally and unbelatedly, to hold out its hand to the rest of the world and say that we call upon the world to join us in the most momentous and magnificent enterprise in history: a world government. Let us make the proposal in good faith. Those nations which want to remain outside may do so. If they do so, I don't see that we are under the obligation not to go ahead with all the rest of the world. If you say this is too big a step, then I ask you to consider the fate of a man who is seriously ill and the doctor comes and diagnoses advanced pneumonia. He says that very drastic measures must be taken. "I'd like to suggest," he says, "that we prescribe one million units of penicillin to be given in doses of one hundred thousand units a day for ten days."

Well, the patient considers this very carefully. He says, "Kind sir, your prescription of one million units of penicillin seems somewhat drastic. At least when you speak in terms of one-hundred-thousand-unit doses. When I survey my life, my upbringing, my education, my training, and my background, my orientation, my philosophy, indeed, I find I couldn't possibly accept so drastic a dose as one hundred thousand units a day for ten days. Therefore, I think I would find it far more convenient and my psyche would certainly respond were you to spread out these doses over a hundred days. Let us say, ten thousand units a day for a hundred days."

The doctor looks at him very carefully and says, "Then, I can see that you are a reasonable man. Very well, I shall give you ten thousand units the first day. And, incidentally, I shall be back tomorrow at three o'clock for the second injection. But I think it is only fair to tell you that the second injection may be somewhat more difficult than the first. You see, it is always more difficult in the presence of rigor mortis."

The world today is calling on you to supply millions upon millions upon millions of units of penicillin, the penicillin of courage, of conscience, of intelligence, of leadership, and is calling upon you, not only to prescribe the dose but to administer it.

Arthur Sylvester

THERE ARE MANY lengthy and learned interpretations of democracy and of communism. But as a primer for laymen the discourse that follows will prove enlightening. It is deceptively simple. It is in fact the clear distillation of a lifetime spent in probing, as a newspaperman, the meaning behind the terms that are most glibly used in describing present-day ideologies. The terms are here stripped of bias and verbiage.

Arthur Sylvester, long associated with the *Newark Evening News,* has been its Washington correspondent since 1944. His conclusion is that totalitarianism "is the true challenge of both the shadow and substance of communism in the Western world," and that we can't rest on our American accomplishments of the past to solve it.

As a study in definition it is important. As informed commentary, it makes an excellent link between the essays that precede and follow it.

T. H. J.

THE SHADOW OF COMMUNISM IN THE WESTERN WORLD

by Arthur Sylvester

W E ARE INCLINED today, in our calmer moments, to regard with ironic amusement Russia's claims to being a democracy. What the members of the Politburo constantly refer to as Soviet democracy, we characterize as Communist totalitarianism. Our disenchantment with Soviet professions in the light of Soviet actions since the end of the war is a natural corollary of our assumption that democracy has reached its final flowering among us.

But this is a poor frame of national mind to cope with a people convinced that they, not we, embody the fruition of the ideas to which we unhesitatingly lay a monopolistic claim. If we are to deal successfully with what has been called the shadow of communism on the Western world, we must understand the basis of Russian claims to being a democracy. Only through such understanding can we hope to compete with the Soviet in the market place of ideas.

The words "democratic," "liberty," and "independence" were constantly on the lips of Russian leaders during World War II. At successive conferences of the Big Three, Marshal Stalin was in the forefront in subscribing to the beauty of democracy. At Yalta, when the Big Three revealed their intention of dealing with political and economic problems of liberated Europe in accordance with democratic principles, Stalin subscribed to the idea that the Polish government was to be reorganized on a "broader democratic basis"—oh, familiar phrase!

Years ago Lenin had said, "Proletarian democracy is a million times more democratic than any bourgeois democracy. The Soviet power is a million times more democratic than the most democratic bourgeois republic." That means the United States.

He said also, "The Soviet system is the maximum of democracy for the workers and peasants. At the same time it means a break with bourgeois democracy and the rise of a new universal historical type of democracy, namely, proletarian democracy or the dictatorship of the proletariat."

His thoughts were echoed in 1936 by Stalin who described the new Soviet constitution as the only thoroughly democratic constitution in the world. Our American reaction today at best is to write off such expressions as propaganda. But we would do well to look, and look again, at what the Russians are talking about when they claim to be proponents of democracy.

Our democracy, which is essentially British in origin, stresses the right to dissent and the rule of law. The former means the protection of minorities; the latter means enforcement of the rights of the individual against the State. From this has flowed our feeling that democratic government means weak government and that the less government there is, the more democracy we will have.

But Soviet democracy derives from the French tradition where the revolution did not result in a balance, or compromise, between the rights of the individual against both the feudalism of the Church and State. The French victory was not for political toleration, but rather for a particular view of the authority of the State. It substituted popular for royal sovereignty. It gave the people the powers formerly enjoyed by the Crown, without challenging or questioning the powers in themselves. The Soviet revolution stems, then, from the French not the English.

Now, it is the Soviet view that the middle class became frightened at the ultimate revolutionary aspirations of the masses and ceased to be revolutionary. We, in the West, they say, stopped short with political democracy and refused to carry through to the logical end, which is social democracy, meaning socialism or communism, a task which they have completed.

In doing so they have presented capitalist democracy with some challenges. In effect they say that Western democracy remains formal and institutional and ignores the class content of the State. Well, obviously they haven't read the Federalist Papers. These show that the framers of our Constitution were acutely conscious that clashing economic interests would create classes in this country too.

But the Soviet leaders also charge that our democracy remains purely political and does not extend to the social and economic phase. They assert it lacks positive belief in itself and is therefore dangerously tolerant of opposition. Finally, they declare that it makes no provision for the participation of the masses in administration.

In essence, the question raised by Soviet democracy is whether the toleration of dissentient opinions, which we declare to be the heart of democracy, means toleration of all dissentient opinions, even those hostile to democracy, or whether it means toleration of dissentient opinions on specific issues among those who accept the fundamentals of democracy. We, as a people, are at the moment debating this question. The activities of Congressman Thomas's Un-American Activities Committee are one form the debate is taking. The curious thing is that his committee and Thomas himself seem to hold with the Soviet view that the democrat who believes that democracy requires equal toleration for opinions both favorable and hostile to democracy is actually guilty of weakness and a faltering faith in democracy.

Communism in its theoretic form is certainly not new in the world. What is new is the dynamic expression of it that has been growing up during the last thirty years in Russia. There it has taken the form of a dictatorship of the proletariat, which manages all productive capital through a centralized state. The mere existence of such a form of government in the heart land of Europe would not necessarily in itself, we assume, constitute anything except an entirely different form of government from ours. We have lived in the world before with governments alien in every way to the American, with only the normal diplomatic strains to irk us. Formulators of American foreign policy and Joseph Stalin, too, have stated repeatedly that the American form of democracy and the Soviet type of democracy can live peacefully in the same world; one does not exclude the other, the leaders of both countries claim.

What, then, causes the conflict? It seems to me it is the Communists' dogmatic belief—and don't forget they may be right—in the inevitable decay of our capitalistic system. They say that that decay, with a consequent collapse, due either to a glut of goods resulting in world-wide depression and unemployment, or to an aggressive war, is inevitable.

This crisis *must* develop, they say, because the continued exploitation of the masses of wage earners by the capitalist leadership can result only in the overthrow of the latter. When that happens there will be established a dictatorship of the proletariat, or, that is, of the masses of people to prevent a counterrevolution by the middle classes.

Unless we keep this Soviet conception firmly fixed in our minds, we can neither understand what makes the Kremlin tick, nor judge properly the appeal that communism has for all sorts of people in our own country, in Latin America, and in Western Europe.

I do not know whether this Soviet analysis of our state as capitalist is correct. But I believe we have not yet had the question put to us in this country in its ultimate and conclusive form. It came very near reaching that stage in 1932. I suspect that in your lifetime the real test case will come. At the moment, with full production and sixty million persons working, it probably seems a remote contingency. But if your generation goes along from year to year in a sort of intellectual twilight sleep, it will be entirely unprepared for the question and the answer when, as they must inevitably do, they confront you. I am convinced that until we do have a final demonstration one way or the other—and I do not mean by war—that the Soviet theory of capitalist democracy is wrong so far as it applies to the West, the shadow of communism will always be upon us in either greater or lesser length.

Too little attention has been paid to the attraction for

many people of the highest principle that lies in this Communist dogma of inevitable capitalist downfall, to the idea that our system bears within it the seeds of its own death. Injected into the struggle of the common man to improve his own lot, this idea has given dynamic fervor to those who embrace the Communist faith.

There is no doubt that it is a faith—indeed a religion—that shows all the proselyting energy and vitality of belief which characterized the early Christian martyrs and which, sad to say, has largely gone out of the Christian religion today. The Kingdom of God, you will recall, is not guaranteed in this life to Christians, and there is nothing inevitable about the attainment of heaven, even for those who struggle mightily. But the Communist religion says that the great body of men will inevitably come into their own on this earth within a reasonable time merely by infiltrating, dividing, and destroying the present form of capitalist democracy.

Faith in this concept on the part of the conspirators was one of the most startling aspects of the Canadian Communist spy case. The Royal Commission in Canada attempted to get at the reasons that induced citizens of a democracy to adopt the Communist philosophy and to work consciously for Communist ends, indeed for the benefit of a foreign and unfriendly party. They were tremendously impressed with the uncanny success with which the Soviet agents who made up the fifth column were able to find Canadians willing to betray their country in the face of all sorts of oaths of allegiance, and all sorts of oaths of office which they had taken.

The Canadians implicated were persons of marked

ability and intelligence, yet the evidence showed that, in the great majority of cases, the motivation was always linked with courses of psychological development that were carried on under the guise of what was ostensibly a legitimate Canadian political organ but was actually a secret Soviet cell embodied in that body. Indoctrination courses were successful in selling the idea that loyalty and obedience to the leadership of the party took precedence over loyalty to Canada, entitled the conspirators to disregard their oath of allegiance and secrecy and so destroy their integrity as citizens under the present Canadian system. It was found in Canada that some of the agents began their Communist associations because of a burning desire to reform and improve Canadian society. The Communist program for social reform in Canada attracted them.

The original motivation was basically ideological. Initially, financial incentive played no part in the case of those who became spies. Later the Soviet agents induced most of them to accept small sums of money and give receipts, receipts that bound them irrevocably to the spy ring. It turned out that the Russian spies didn't know when they had a good thing, because it was through receipts that members of the ring were disclosed.

Other studies have shown that communism in the last twenty-five years has become a new form of idealism for some persons, and a substitute for religion to others. In considering the latter group it is interesting to note that among the most prominent apostates from communism today are men who joined the party as apostates originally from the Roman Catholic faith. The Communist movement has provided an outlet for rebels against one or another form of exploitation, for members of minority groups, acutely conscious of discrimination against them, and for intellectuals and others with a strong will to remake this sorry world in which we live.

The shadow of communism has lain across the Western world ever since the Bolshevik Revolution of 1919. It will be with us for years to come, and we had better be prepared to live with it. It has been alternately heavier or lighter as the shrewd men in the Kremlin have applied more or less pressure against the capitalist democracy in line with their concept that those democracies must eventually fall.

After the democracies achieved victory in 1918, they suddenly suffered a loss of faith in their potential, just when they seemed to be at the height of their power. In many parts of the world they were abandoned in favor of other forms of government that promised solutions to social and economic problems, forms of government that have disappeared, some of them quite recently.

During the thirties when democracies, particularly ours, reeled under economic misfortune, the Communist pressure mounted again. It is significant that the best showing the American Communist party ever made politically was in 1932 when William Z. Foster polled a hundred and three thousand votes as a presidential candidate. That was the peak, and it has never been approached since, and we haven't had a depression like that since, either.

Today, although once again victorious over their enemies, the Western European democracies find the tide of faith in them ebbing. At times some of us here act as if we, too, didn't really believe in the American people, simply because certain of our fellow countrymen are not convinced that this nation has achieved the social and economic democracy we have a right to expect along with our political democracy.

The important fact is that the Kremlin looks out on the disarranged world of the capitalist democracies and finds the prospect good—good, that is, for accelerating their downfall. So once again, since chaos is their business, the Communists are putting on the pressure in the hope that their time is at hand.

There is always the possibility of a resort to arms to settle what is basically an ideological conflict. This would be an admission that we have no other solution for the current crisis of Western civilization, which, in reality, is the crisis of the individual. In this country we are committed to the belief that the individual mind and heart of each one of us is the final human repository of truth and that each must make his own judgments.

Totalitarianism, whether it be of the medieval church and empire, which we threw off, or whether it be of the modern Soviet brand, contends, on the contrary, that some church, or some governments, or some party has the correct and ultimate access to truth. That being so, totalitarianism claims the right and duty of impressing the individuals of society with its revelations in any way likely to prove effective.

This is the true challenge of both the shadow and substance of communism in the Western world, and war won't solve it. That is a task for members of the Lawrenceville student body and their contemporaries, in the coming years. You're going to need friends all over the world to resolve what is clearly a conflict of basic ideals. You can't rest on our American accomplishments of the past. You will have to attract new adherents by devising enlarged social and economic programs to allow for what is valid in Soviet democracy and at the same time to preserve the values of capitalist democracy.

Eduard C. Lindeman

SINCE 1924, Eduard C. Lindeman has been professor of social philosophy at the New York School of Social Work in Columbia University. He has written authoritatively in the broad field of human relations because he has drawn on his lifetime studies. In this essay he says, "I wish to devote special attention to . . . the relation between American education and what I am pleased to call the democratic disciplines."

To that end, aware that "only in static societies is it possible to maintain a regimented and uniform system of education," he attacks four major problems that confront the American people: the place of private schools and colleges, the role of general education, the question of religious teaching in public schools, and the right of pupils to discuss controversial questions.

T. H. J.

EDUCATION FOR A NEW DEMOCRATIC ERA

by *Eduard C. Lindeman*

W E LIVE IN A time of contentiousness. Our world is in flux. Speaking in broad historical terms it appears that an era has come to an end and that consequently we stand on the threshold of a new age. The voices that speak on behalf of this coming era are divided. The world itself is split into two great camps, and there exists no common understanding. The language of public discourse is harsh, argumentative, accusative.

Under these circumstances it is important that those who speak publicly should say what they mean. We cannot expect agreement but we must strive for clarity. Confusion leads to doubt and doubt to fear. When I contemplate the contemporary mood I am reminded of an occasion that took place almost a century ago. A deep-seated moral issue, slavery, had tormented the American people. Many compromises were proposed and tried, but the underlying moral factor was not candidly confronted. Hence, the moral fiber of the American people showed signs of deterioration. In the midst of this period of confusion and deterioration a series of debates took place in the State of Illinois between Abraham Lincoln and Stephen Douglas. Two intertwined issues constituted the subject matter of these debates, namely, the preservation of the Union and slavery. Lincoln had come to the conclusion that the Union

63

could not be saved with slavery, but his principal cause was the Union. In one of these debates Judge Douglas attempted to confuse the audience by twisting Lincoln's words about in such manner as to make it appear that he had not meant what he said and that what he said about slavery in particular was not what he really meant. While this exercise in confusion was in process, Mr. Lincoln sat in the shadow of the platform with his head resting in his hands and obviously in sorrow. Finally, the chairman called upon him for a final rebuttal. Mr. Lincoln was so engrossed that he did not hear. He was called a second and a third time, and at last he arose, walked slowly to the edge of the platform, and addressed his audience in this language:

> My fellow citizens: I am not a master of language; I have not a fine education; I am not capable of engaging into a disquisition upon dialectics, as I believe you call it; but I do not believe the language I employed bears any such construction as Judge Douglas puts upon it. But I don't care to quibble in regard to words. I know what I meant, and I will not leave this crowd in doubt, if I can explain to them what I really meant in the use of that paragraph.*

I like to believe that this stand of Lincoln's was the beginning of a moral reawakening among the American people. They thereupon found the courage to face their fundamental issue, and even though it led straight to tragedy, they did face it.

---

* Quoted by Bliss Perry in *The American Mind,* Houghton, Mifflin, Boston, Mass., 1912.

Today's issue is equally imbued with moral elements. Our choice is between a democratic way of life in which certain human and social values are embedded and a totalitarian way of life which negates those values. My faith and hope are attached to democracy, but I am fully aware that we cannot go back to democratic ways that were once sufficient but on the contrary we must move forward into a new democratic era. You may not agree with all that I have to say about the democracy of the future. I do not ask for agreement. In fact, it is my conviction that too much agreement is dangerous to a democratic people. What I do plead for with all the earnestness at my command is that you shall participate in the discussions pertaining to the democratic struggle of our time.

Whatever else may be said about the democratic way of life in any era is the fact that democracy and education are inseparable. Where the people are consulted, where the governed are also the governors, the people must be informed. They must be so educated as to realize their responsibilities and duties. The price they must pay for the freedom democracy grants is informed citizenship. It is important therefore that young men who are enjoying the benefits of education should be asked to consider their democratic responsibilities.

There will always be an educational issue. In a dynamic society the time will never come when there will be universal agreement respecting either the ends or the means of learning. Only in static societies is it possible to maintain a regimented and uniform system of education. If civilization itself is changing, then education must also change. Otherwise there will be stagnation and decay. Ours is most certainly a changing civilization, and consequently it is to be expected that education will continue to be a live social issue.

Among the various educational questions that now confront the American people, I shall select the following for briefer treatment:

(a) What is the place of private schools and colleges in a democratic society?

(b) Why is a general education essential for citizens of a democracy?

(c) Should religion be taught in the public schools?

(d) Should younger pupils be expected to discuss controversial questions as a part of their general education?

These questions have been selected because these are at the moment issues concerning which the American people are agitated. These are the questions that are now being debated in both public and private assemblies, and I have no doubt that you have already considered each of them in the course of recent discussions. I shall not attempt to be judicious or comprehensive with respect to these questions because I wish to devote special attention to still another, namely, the relation between American education and what I am pleased to call the democratic disciplines. My chief intent with respect to the four issues listed above is to precipitate earnest reflection on your part. I shall in each instance state my own convictions but this does not mean that I am right and all who disagree are wrong. It merely implies that I have come to certain conclusions, and if you will begin your reflections by assuming a critical attitude toward my conclusions, I shall feel certain that an educational process has begun among you.

The place of private schools in a democracy

Private schools and colleges, as well as private social agencies, are involved in a struggle for survival. During the past two decades there has been a marked tendency to place the burden of education and social welfare on governmental agencies. During this same period there has been a gradual increase in taxation and a lowering of income from investments, thus making it increasingly difficult for institutions dependent on endowments to maintain standards and expand. Because of these facts many persons have come to believe that the day of private institutions, especially private schools, will soon be over. This, then, is one of the issues which the American people will need to resolve.

My conviction respecting this question rests on the assumption that when in any society all primary functions are performed by the government and no room is left for private initiative and action democracy will already have ceased to exist. When all basic activities are controlled and regulated by governmental agencies it becomes impossible to retain those fundamental freedoms upon which the democratic ideal rests, and without freedom it is meaningless to speak as though democracy existed. This does not mean that there will not be a steady increase in governmental operations and controls, but it does mean that a democratic government will always stop short of complete control. Believing that private institutions are integral to a democratic society, it thereupon becomes necessary to ask: Under what conditions will it be possible to maintain strong private institutions in the United States? The general answer to this question hinges, of course, upon the will of the people with respect to private institutions. If the people do not realize the worth and strategy of maintaining private institutions for the sake of retaining democracy, then no satisfactory answer to my question will be found, and such institutions will ultimately disappear. But, aside from this general response, private institutions must face the fact that they will need to relate themselves dynamically to the democratic ideal if they expect approval and survival. Private schools, for example, must rid themselves of the stigma of being class-conscious institutions with a snob appeal. They must learn to practice democracy both internally and externally, both with respect to teachers and students and the public. The price which private institutions must pay in order to subsist within democratic societies is this: they must serve democratic aspirations. They must also give assurances that the quality of work they perform is of high order. They may remain outside of bureaucratic control provided they contribute a proper quota of diversity within the field they represent.

Why is general education essential for citizens of a democracy?

The current debate between advocates of general versus vocational education is in one sense of those confusing "either-ors" that take on meaning only when the "versus" is omitted. Both types of education are needed in modern societies. We need to learn how to make a living as well as how to live well and purposefully. The person who lacks skills is a misfit in a technological age. But the person with skills, the trained artisan or professional, needs also to know something else if he is to be an active and useful participant in a democratic setting. He needs to know how to deal with questions of value, and this facility is the product of general education.

In modern life the sources of value are multiple, not singular. We seek our values in religion, in science, in literature, the arts, secular philosophy, and in the ideals set for us by the ideological pattern within which we live. In order to be able to tap these various sources of value we must be equipped with a general background, an education that is humane rather than technical. The citizen who at an early age is shunted off into specialized vocational education is still required to make important decisions involving values. Without a general education he suffers a serious handicap. It is for this reason that all citizens of a democracy should receive, whether in school or out, a general education.

Should religion be taught in or under the auspices of public schools?

It is one of the curious anomalies of our age that this question should have become a burning issue. Our forefathers may have thought that this issue was definitely and once and for all settled by the constitutional provision that has in the past been assumed to declare for a sharp separation of Church and State. But there are now some eighteen separate states of the Union where religion in some form or other is being taught under the auspices of, or with the co-operation of, public schools.

As is true of most fundamental problems under our form of constitutional government, this question will eventually be resolved by the Supreme Court. In the meantime it will continue to be a topic for lively debate. The movement to utilize the public schools for religious instruction is, I believe, founded upon a serious error. Parents and religious leaders who have given assent to this dangerous intermixture of religion and government have been misled, so I believe, by a confusion of desires. What they really wanted at the outset was moral instruction. They had become alarmed over increases in juvenile delinquency and had come to feel that the public schools had a responsibility for teaching morals. But the schools were not prepared to teach morality, and hence it was assumed that the easiest and simplest formula for teaching morals was to begin by teaching theology. There is no way, so far as I know, of teaching theology without a bias, that is, without a sectarian emphasis. By what right, then, does the public school arrogate to itself the privilege of indoctrinating pupils with sectarian religious beliefs? It is clear that I am opposed to this tendency, and my reasons are manifold, but not the least important of my reasons is my strong feeling that this procedure will in the end do great harm to religion. Finally, churches will be obliged to cater to politicians and at this juncture religion will already have ceased to be free.

Should younger pupils be expected to discuss controversial questions as a part of their general education?

When this question is debated in parent-teacher meetings and at forums emphasis is always placed upon the word "controversial." It is thus made to appear that here are two types of issues, some of which are to be labeled controversial and others innocent or nondebatable. Apparently, young pupils are to be allowed to discuss the

70

innocent issues but are to be shielded from controversial ones. I seem to detect a propaganda device in the way in which this question is posed. All issues are controversial. That is what makes them issues. If there were no differences of opinion, there would be no issues. The word "controversial" is inserted in this equation for purposes of frightening parents and teachers. By this simple procedure it thus becomes possible to exclude from school discussion all of the very questions which are important and about which there is disagreement. And thus it happens that schools become shelters from reality. It is probable that this type of protectiveness accounts for the fact that so few of the citizens who pass through our public schools avail themselves of the opportunity of voting at elections.*

It seems to me both pedagogically and ethically sound to permit the full and frank discussion of all questions among younger pupils at the time their interest is aroused. When the adult postpones such discussions he exposes himself. He runs the risk that the pupil will discuss the problem in any case but in all likelihood without guidance, or he leads the pupil to believe that it is he, the adult, who is not prepared to enter upon a candid discussion of significant questions.

The above issues do not by any means exhaust the list of basic questions which are at the moment agitating the minds of earnest Americans who care about education. Many are deeply concerned over the question of racial

---

* Slightly more than half of the eligible voters voted in the 1948 presidential election. In a recent statement Harold Stassen asserted that only sixty per cent of the graduates of American colleges and universities voted in this same election.

segregation in American schools and colleges. The Supreme
Court has said that educational segregation is not un-
constitutional provided the segregated pupils receive an
education that is equal to that of the nonsegregated.* But
where does one find such equality? Certainly not in the
Southern states where segregation is universally practiced.
Some private schools have begun to realize that they too
may have a responsibility in this connection, and here and
there one now finds interesting experiments of interracial
education.

It will be observed by scrutinizing the above issues that
in each instance there is a definite democratic relation. In
each case the issue might have been prefaced with the
clause *"in a democratic society should...,"* etc. In other
words, the chief questions in American education seem to
revolve about the more fundamental question, which is:
What kind of education is most suitable for a nation that
is by affirmation and aspiration democratic? We cannot
answer this question until we have a clearer notion concerning the meaning of democracy.

*Are there some common denominators upon which we can
agree?*

Before approaching this last-named question, it seems
pertinent to me to ask whether in all this welter of disagreement and contention there are a few educational
items about which one might expect a high degree of

* My frequent references to the Supreme Court of the United States
are not accidental. One way of distinguishing between basic and secondary
issues in American life is to observe which ones continue to arrive before
the Supreme Court, for this means that the Constitution is either silent or
ambiguous about these questions, and hence these must be resolved by
judicial decisions.

concurrence. If so, our task will be made somewhat lighter. May we, for example, agree that education should deal with the growth of the total person, his physical, emotional, social as well as intellectual development? If the role of modern education is comprehensive in this sense, then we shall at least have one guidepost by which to steer our course. May we agree that it is the function of modern education to bring pupils into contact with reality? And should we include in our conception of reality various social problems that make our democracy so vulnerable? May we also agree that there is need for educational institutions that will produce scholars as well as institutions which will train students to be useful and productive workers and technicians? And, finally, may we agree that in every educational institution there should be a heavy emphasis upon training for citizenship? It seems to me that I do encounter a high level of agreement respecting the above questions among American citizens and educators, and with these agreements in mind I now address myself to the last, namely, preparation for democratic citizenship.

The nature of the democratic disciplines

In 1945 while I was acting as educational adviser to the British Army in Occupied Germany, I made an attempt to teach democracy to a group of adolescent German boys who had received a thorough Nazi indoctrination in all their previous education. I began by telling them that democracy means liberty, equality, fraternity, dignity for individuals, government by law instead of by men, etc., etc., but long before I had completed the list of these idealistic eighteenth-century democratic values, I was aware of the fact that my audience was dissenting. They finally interrupted in a very rude manner and said they were unwilling to listen to this type of interpretation of democracy. They insisted that these values represented the false façade of democracy and that they knew full well that equality does not prevail in America, nor is freedom granted to all, and they were entirely certain that hatreds are to be found among American citizens. As we discussed their objections, it slowly dawned upon me that there was some justice in the harsh judgments of these unmannerly Nazi youths. They made me realize that modern democracy stands in need of another set of values, principles that can be validated in part at least by science and in part by experience. We need not forsake the older ideals. They will continue to guide us and give us a sense of direction, but if we are to teach democracy to a new generation, we must utilize values that have a more practical meaning. It was this realization which forced me to undertake the project of examining the democratic experience in order to discover what values had been precipitated, not as preconceived ideals but, rather, as ways of living that grew directly from the "soil" of democratic experience. I call these newer values "empirical," meaning thereby that they are susceptible to tests, and I shall now proceed to furnish a few examples, which I trust you will discuss further.

What discipline of life is required of those who claim membership in a democratic society? How are such persons to behave? The word "discipline" as used here implies control from within rather than from without. The discipline required of citizens of a totalitarian society is obedience to rulers. By contrast, the discipline of democratic citizens is self-imposed. They behave according to rules they themselves have formulated and which they believe to be right and good.

In a democracy it is assumed, for example, that diversity is superior to uniformity. The motto of our nation is *E Pluribus Unum* which may be translated to mean "through diversity toward unity." Why not strive for unity by means of uniformity? What special virtue attaches to the conception of difference, variety, or diversity? And, is it true that the doctrine of diversity is supported by scientific evidence? These are questions most Americans have never asked, and hence they have not been satisfactorily answered.

In the beginning this diversity principle was applied primarily to government. Our forefathers designed a system of government in which power was to be divided in such manner as to prevent its concentration in either the executive, the judicial, or the legislative branches. In this manner it was hoped that such degrees of centralized power as might lead to dictatorship would be prevented. This hope has been for the most part justified. We still live under a government of checks and balances, and we have thus far avoided the threat of dictatorship either through an authoritative executive or bureaucratic officials. But if this principle is sound politically and thus provides us with certain guarantees of freedom, why is it not also applicable to other spheres of life? It is true that most Americans believe that the principle of diversity applies to religion. We do not desire an official state religion. To a certain extent we also adhere to the diversity rule with respect to the various cultural groups that combine to form our population. In this sphere, however, we have in recent years discovered some disturbing exceptions. Anti-Semitism represents, perhaps, the most serious rift in the American belief that people have a right to be different. If we honestly believed in cultural pluralism (diversity of population), we would, of course, be extremely proud of the fact that there are in America some twelve million Negroes, some five million Jews, three million Mexicans, and a scattering of Orientals. We would anticipate that each of these cultural groups would have a special gift to bring to the nation, and we would insist that they must be free to make their contributions.

The time has come when we must also test this principle in the realm of economics. Economic discussions usually proceed on the assumption that only two choices are available, namely, private enterprise on the one hand and state socialism or communism on the other. But there seems to me to be a strong reason for believing that in a democracy the choice will ultimately be less simple. In order to sustain our freedom and at the same time maintain high productive levels, we may be required to experiment with a plural economy, that is, a mixed economy in which varieties of enterprise work side by side and on behalf of the same goals.

Hitler violated this basic democratic doctrine of diversity when he attempted to create a nation based on sameness rather than difference. His aim was to create a German state in which all people belonged to the same racial stock. He eliminated distinctions between political parties. He created a propaganda machine for the purpose of making all Germans think alike, and he brought into existence a ruthless police system to punish those who dared to differ. Through these various efforts at creating unity through uniformity Hitler created a powerful state, so powerful that he felt certain it could conquer the free, democratic nations. Happily, we defeated his plans but the cost was tremendous, and not the least of the price we have had to pay is the fact that totalitarianism spread widely the seeds of skepticism regarding democracy. And now we find ourselves confronted with another monolithic state, another nation in which diversity is outlawed and uniformity is extolled, namely, Soviet Russia.

If, then, we really believe in democracy, we must devote ourselves to a thorough-going examination of the principle of diversity. We must ask more earnestly than we have done before why diversity and freedom seem to be interrelated. But above all, we must learn how to teach this principle by both precept and example until there is no longer any doubt among the majority of American citizens that we can achieve a higher strength in this manner than is possible through uniformity and totalitarianism.

Over and over the citizen of a democracy must ask himself why he is so frequently called upon to *live with decisions that have gone against him*. There is an election, and the contending parties make extravagant claims for the rightness of their position and the wrongness of their opponents'. They threaten the nation with dire disaster if they are not put into office. And then the people vote. They make a decision. Sometimes the vote is overwhelmingly in favor of one party or one set of candidates, and at other times the decision is extremely close. In both instances, however, after the votes have been counted, the people's verdict is accepted. The same is true when the

77

Supreme Court hands down an important decision. Once the decision has become the law of the land, the citizen accepts it and orders his life accordingly. Why do we accept decisions which are contrary to our wishes and perhaps to our personal interests?

It may be argued that we accept contrary decisions merely on grounds of sportsmanship. We have been taught that to be a good loser is in itself a moral virtue, a sign of high moral character. (Incidentally, when I discussed this principle with German youth in 1945 I discovered that there is no German word for sportsmanship. One partial equivalent exists but it applies only to hunting.) I accept this explanation in part. To be a citizen of a democratic nation calls for the quality of sportsmanship. But I am convinced that there are even more fundamental reasons to explain why the art of living with decisions that go against you is one that needs to be acquired by all who subscribe to democracy. This deeper reason is to be found, I believe, in the theory of minorities. We obey the rule of majorities, not because we are convinced that majorities must always be right but because we know that in no other way can freedom be preserved. Hence we grant special privileges to minorities. Minorities are protected by the Constitution itself. What we have still to learn concerning this belief that minorities are to be cherished is the art of living creatively as a member of a minority group.

A minority person may choose one of three courses: (a) He may withdraw; he may say, "I'll not play if I can't have my way." This is obviously an immature attitude. (b) He may remain within the organization in which he finds himself in the minority but he may also say, "Very well, I have been defeated but from now onward I shall see that the majority's decisions do not prevail; I shall sabotage." This is also the attitude of an immature person but it is besides slightly sinister. (c) The minority person may, in the third place, decide to remain a participant, insist that the majority decision be given a fair trial, and at the same time continue to explore and experiment with the notion in which he still believes but which had been rejected by the majority. This seems to me to be the attitude of a mature person, but it appears to be also the only workable procedure for keeping democracy alive.

Many of our finest citizens have not yet learned the democratic rule that assumes that in a democracy one must never expect more than a *partial fulfillment of ideals*. Perfectionism and democracy are incompatibles. In a totalitarian society one may take the all-or-none position. There one may ask for a completely radical step in a given direction. But in a democracy one can move ahead only one step at a time. Why? Why should democracies be thus handicapped? Why cannot we also claim the whole realization of our ideals? There are numerous ways of answering these questions but the one which must be fairly obvious is this: In a democracy whatever decision is reached must carry along not merely those who were its proponents but also those who opposed it; in other words, wherever the rule of diversity applies, there can be nothing more than a partial realization of ideals. If the entire step is taken at once, too many persons with shades of difference will be left behind, excluded. The consent of the governed is a principle that implies that the governed have a right to differ. When, as often happens in totalitarian nations, the people humbly accept the command of the dictator, they are not consenting; they are merely acquiescing. We can consent provided we do not strain the rule of preserving minorities or violate the principle of diversity.

I come now to one of the most difficult of the democratic disciplines as well as one of the oldest and most persistent philosophical problems. In a democracy we insist that *ends and the means must be so far as possible compatible.* Defendants of so-called Eastern or Russian democracy declare that any action is democratic if it is in the interest of all the people. We, the inheritors of so-called Western democracy, insist on the contrary that the action must also be taken *by* the people and must be a function *of* the people. Why do we insist so stubbornly that democracy is both means and ends, method and goal? Why do we assert that it is impossible to attain good ends through the use of undesirable means?

Our answers to these questions are at one and the same time scientific and moral. We believe that the means must be in harmony with the ends because we also believe that science teaches that we become what we do. To anticipate good results from faulty methods is, in other words, an unscientific belief. Our moral reasoning is based on the assumption that those who violate the principle of compatibility between means and ends sooner or later become so careless concerning their means that they finally take on the pattern of conspiratorial behavior. Those who do not test their means as well as their ends become manipulators. Corruption lies concealed in every person and in every movement in which the achievement of ends, no matter how good, is attempted through the instrumentality of means that are in themselves a denial of the ends proposed. In one sense, this incongruity represents one of the most tragic aspects of the Soviet State. It is utterly unthinkable that the Soviet Union will ever achieve the lofty goals the leaders so loudly proclaim if they continue to utilize brutal, nonhumane, and tyrannical means.

I have now furnished illustrations of four democratic disciplines, four rules of conduct that citizens of a democracy must learn and exemplify, namely: (a) the rule of diversity, (b) the rule of living with decisions that go against you, (c) the principle of partial realizations of ideals, and (d) the law of compatibility between means and ends. These are samples of what I have called "empirical democratic values," and I now ask you to consider these disciplines thoughtfully and critically. Ask yourselves as candidly as possible how these rules apply to your life at school, your life in the home, your associations with your fellows, and finally your membership in a democratic community. Find out whether or not these rules are supported by scientific evidence. Examine the outcomes of situations in which these rules are either obeyed or flouted. By this process you will become honest and, I believe, more devoted interpreters of the democratic way of life.

And while you are engaged in this democratic adventure, may I also hope that you will continue to use the perspective of humor. The struggle for democracy appears at times to be fraught with a grim kind of seriousness. But I am convinced that the final victory will go, not to the grim and the humorless but rather to the gay and the gallant. For humor rests on solid grounds. It springs from confidence. Humor provides a kernel of truth to situations confused and frightening. As the totalitarians become more grim and forbidding, let us demonstrate our faith in democracy through our continuing capacity to derive fun from the struggle. The free should also be happy.

Charles W. Cole

For those who want a view of the workings of the actual machinery of peacetime, which manufacture the conditions by which wars become inevitable or by which they may be averted, the essay that follows is an authoritative exposition. Do not decide before you read it that you think the subject of economic nationalism is either abstruse or dull. You will here discover in the skillful hands of an expert that the subject can be fascinating. An ardent free-trader, Charles Woolsey Cole was a professor of economics at Amherst College from 1937 to 1940, and he has been president of the institution since 1946. During the intervening seven years he served as professor of history at Columbia University.

"I cannot but believe," he concludes in his essay, "whatever the administration and whatever the conditions of prosperity or depression that we will not try to maintain this freer trade and work for peace and prosperity by removing the economic barriers that separate one nation from another."

T. H. J.

ECONOMIC NATIONALISM
AND WORLD TRADE

by Charles W. Cole

NATIONALISM IN ITSELF is something that you are all familiar with. It is very hard to define because it is partly patriotism, and it is partly a feeling of belonging to a country. It is partly a feeling of being willing to work for it—and even to die for it. Nationalism is to a very large degree political, and cannot exist until nations are organized for action in the political sphere. But there is also economic nationalism, and that is a very old and very important subject.

In the Middle Ages, say in the twelfth century, it would have been difficult for anybody to think of a person living a few miles away from him as being completely outside of his own economic sphere. People thought of those close to them as related to them. But in the seventeenth century and thereafter, there were drawn boundary lines that separated people, stopped their trade, and cut off their economic interests, until a situation was created such that people living on one side of the line frequently thought of those on the other side of the line as economic enemies— ones whom they should hurt in trade, rather than help. And such a feeling is one phase of economic nationalism.

Economic nationalism can be seen in three main areas. One, a country inside itself tries to control its economic life, its business, its industry, its trade, so as to make the country wealthy and strong and prosperous. A second field on which we could spend much time is "imperialism." Imperialism means seeking for colonies where goods can be sold, raw materials secured, and investments made. It is another phase of economic nationalism.

But the earliest phase and the easiest to discuss is the question of trade barriers, these fences that we build up between people, which prevent goods flowing back and forth between them. The barriers are usually called "tariffs." They can be quotas, or import controls, or exchange restrictions, but the tariff is the typical barrier. It is usually a tax or import duty charged on goods brought into a country. If it is merely a tax, it does not matter very much. But it is usually used to keep out foreign competition from the home market and to build up home industry.

Now, there is a very interesting pattern on the development of tariffs in European history. If you start out about 1600 you find that these economic barriers, these import duties, were rather low. Today we would consider them ridiculously low. From about 1600 to about 1850 they tended to rise steadily higher and higher and higher. Though still, in 1850, we would have considered them from today's point of view moderate. Then there came a movement in the other direction. It began in the 1840's or a little earlier in England and it culminated about 1870. In that period the tariffs tended to go down steadily, until they reached their low point in the 1860's. At that time nations were trading more freely with each other, buying goods from, and selling them to, various foreign peoples more freely than they ever have, before or since, in modern history. From 1870 on, the tariffs rose steadily until 1939 when they, together with other trade barriers, had reached tremendous heights, and trade was being throttled down to a scanty trickle among all the peoples of the world.

Now if you ask why tariffs rose for two hundred and fifty years and then sank for thirty or forty years and then rose again until very recently, no clear response is possible. I once sat down and tried to work out all the different possible answers, and I made up at least twelve that seemed to make some sense. But then I decided that none of them were really complete or correct solutions of the problem. Three of the twelve will serve as samples of the kind of answers that can be given.

One of them is that the whole problem has to do in a very complicated way with the amount of gold in the world. There was not enough gold from 1600 to 1848. Then, the discovery of gold just a hundred years ago in California gave people more money, more metallic currency. This trend was reinforced by gold discoveries in Australia and Canada. The increased supply of money loosened credit and made businessmen more venturesome. It gave them a period of prosperity and rising prices. As long as there was an increasing supply of gold, good times continued, tensions relaxed, and trade was more free. Then by 1873 the gold ran short again. Depression and hard times returned. There was a period of rising tariffs, checked briefly in 1896 by the cyanide process for treating gold ores, which was discovered and applied in South Africa. But business expanded more rapidly than the gold supply, and hard times came again after World War I. With hard times came an eagerness to "protect" the home markets, and this was done by raising tariffs.

Another answer that I like better, because it is less complicated, goes something like this. The only country that ever really went in for free trade and actually abolished tariff barriers was England. England had gotten the jump on the rest of the world in the industrial revolution and was so far ahead by 1850 or '60 that other countries could not compete with the English. She could have free trade because nobody could ship manufactures into England when English goods were the cheapest and best in the world. But the English were so powerful and so successful that the other nations copied Britain and thought that her policies must hold the key to prosperity. They therefore reduced their own tariff barriers until it became clear that less advanced countries could not compete successfully with Great Britain. When they realized this fact in the 1870's, all the other countries began raising their tariffs to keep out English goods and encourage their own industries.

But I am afraid that the best answer, the most accurate answer, is that economic nationalism in general and tariffs in particular—the whole policy of trying to make one country strong at the expense of others—are closely connected with war and the threat of war.

During the seventeenth and eighteenth centuries Europe was at war most of the time. It is a fact that between 1689 and 1815 France and England were at war with each other just one half the time. Each European country being involved in war or preparing for war or getting over a war was continually trying to build up its own economy at the expense of other nations.

Then, from 1815 to 1870 there was a period of the most profound peace that Europe has known. It was so prolonged, and people got so used to peace that the Crimean War in far-off Russia on the fringes of civilization scarcely seemed a real interruption of this pacific era. Peace came to seem the normal thing, and people got over worrying about war, got over trying to be ready for war, and began trading with each other freely. They even felt less concern as to whether commerce was strengthening their neighbors as well as themselves. Then the Franco-Prussian War of 1870 and the growth of armies and militarism thereafter started nations competing again in armaments, in navies, and in economic nationalism. Tariff barriers rose once more and grew steadily higher. This trend was confirmed and accentuated by World War I and its aftermath.

There is a quotation that illustrates in striking fashion this view that war and trade are inextricably tied together. It is from a man now rather in disrepute. So much so in fact he should be cited not as an authority but rather as a symptom. The quotation is from Benito Mussolini speaking in 1938. He said:

Now, above all, even those with the thickest brains can see that the division between the economy of peace and the economy of war is simply absurd. There is not an economy for peacetime and an economy for wartime. There is only a war economy, because, historically, considering the number of years of war, it has been demonstrated that a state of armed warfare is a normal state of the people, at least of those living on the European continent, because even in the years of so-called peace other types of war are waged which, in turn, prepare our armed warfare. Therefore, it is the fact or rather the imminent fatality of armed warfare that ought to dominate, and does dominate, our economy.

That is one view. For the opposite view we can cite that given by an Englishman named Richard Cobden, who was perhaps the most earnest advocate of free trade in the mid-nineteenth century. He said: "Free trade is the international law of the Almighty." By that he meant that he thought freer trade among people would bring peace. He argued that there is a relationship between unfree trade, hindered trade, be-tariffed trade, and war, and between free trade and peace. An argument can be made, and I would be prepared to make it, that economic nationalism in the sense of tariffs and trade barriers was a major cause, perhaps *the* major cause, of World War II. One of Wilson's fourteen points was the removal of all economic barriers and the establishment of equality of trade conditions. Of all his fourteen points, that was probably the most thoroughly ignored as the world slid dismally down the slope that led to World War II.

In 1914 there were twenty-two European states. In 1920 there were seven new countries and seven thousand new miles of customs barriers in Europe. The United States perhaps led the way in tariff making, in raising barriers to trade, but England, which had long been the outstanding free-trade country, in 1921 passed a tariff act called the Safeguarding of Industries Act, and France between 1919 and 1922 raised her tariff duties sixty-five times. Hungary fought tariff wars with Czechoslovakia; Rumania and Poland fought tariff wars with Germany; Yugoslavia fought a tariff war with Austria. The whole of the European continent was embroiled in these trade disputes and was cut up commercially among squabbling nations, each of which was trying to build itself up at the expense of the others.

If the 1920's were bad, the 1930's were still worse. The French invented a new device for throttling trade, called "quotas," which provided in effect that no matter what tariff duties paid, the amounts of each type of import were to be strictly limited in quantity. For example, the French would not permit America to send in more than so many thousand dollars' worth of typewriters or so many thousand dollars' worth of automobile tires, no matter what the tariff duty was. In 1932 England laid a general tariff on all her trade, and in the same year in the Ottawa agreements, she put a tariff wall around the whole British Empire with the co-operation of the Dominions. In 1936 Germany invented a new device, which was called the "barter agreement." The tariff barriers had grown so high that nations could not trade with each other. Germany, therefore, instead of trading freely with all countries began making deals with one nation at a time. It would buy the Turkish tobacco crop and promise steel in return. It would buy the Brazilian coffee crop and promise chemicals in return. Since Germany was a very powerful country under Hitler at this time and a very ruthless bargainer, the countries that dealt with her found themselves not infrequently getting the short end of the deal.

Yugoslavia bartered some food products for some chemical goods, and Germany shipped thither a whole trainload of aspirin, which would have cured all the headaches in Yugoslavia for a good many years. And the Yugoslavs had to make the best use of it that they could. An even odder case was that of the Brazilians. They traded coffee for optical goods and the Germans sent them an enormous shipment of glass eyes. The Brazilians do not use large quantities of glass eyes, and to make matters worse, those delivered by the Germans were mostly blue eyes though the Brazilians are almost invariably brown eyed.

Thus it was that trade, which had once been multilateral and fairly free, was in the 1930's held down, and became increasingly bilateral. Great Britain had once paid for her imports from the United States by selling goods to South America, the Balkans, Central Europe, and a dozen other areas. Now she, like Germany, was driven to desperate attempts to make her imports from each nation more or less balance her exports to that country. Trade, which had once flowed freely, was now carried on painfully, bit by bit, shipment by shipment.

Hitler, in the 1930's, said, "Germany must export or die." It was one of the serious facts about Germany's situation that Germany's trade was barred from many colonial overseas areas and from many European areas. Thus the Nazis could argue with conviction that the only way by which Germany could get a decent living was through war. The opportunities for peaceful trade were, they felt, being reduced every day through tariffs. The world-trade situation thus created one of the major arguments that led the Germans on to their mad war of aggression against mankind. Today Britain finds herself in a position even worse than that of Germany in 1936. She must export or starve.

Cobden had said that free trade was the international law of the Almighty. By 1939 there was no free trade and very little international law. The world was ripe for war. And to this state of things economic nationalism with its trade barriers had contributed mightily.

Now, what role did the United States play in all this picture? This is a subject for the most serious examination because in the very near future America is once again going to have to make some crucial decisions on the issue of freer trade.

The role of the United States may be sketched briefly. A hundred years ago today we had what anybody would call a low tariff; it averaged about 22 per cent. We traded freely with the whole world. We pursued a low tariff policy because we were largely an agricultural country, and the manufacturers were not powerful enough to get high tariffs to shut out goods that would compete with those they made. When the Civil War came, the Republicans had just come to power on a platform that had promised the manufacturers of New England and Pennsylvania higher tariff duties to increase their profits. The Republicans lived up to their promise. In 1861 they put through the Morrill Act, which almost doubled our tariff duties. They had a good excuse for it since internal taxes were increasing as the war came on and higher duties on imports could be thought of as creating some equality of conditions for domestic and imported goods. Thus, in a sense, these tariff duties were war taxes, but when the war was over, it was found impossible to remove or lower them. The industries that had made profits under tariff protection and the people who had profited from the existence of the tariff were so powerful that they were able to thwart any movement toward freer international trade. Instead of reducing tariffs the United States maintained them and even raised them slightly, up to 1890 when again, under Republican administration and under the leadership of

McKinley, who later became President, the tariff was raised still further.

Then the Democrats came into power and, after squabbling among themselves endlessly, reduced the tariff a little by the Wilson Act of 1894. But the Republicans, back in the saddle once more, passed the Dingley Act of 1897, which pushed our import duties far higher than they had ever been before. After long and acrimonious political discussions, the Republicans reduced the tariff somewhat by the Payne-Aldrich Act of 1910, and the Democrats pushed it still lower with the Underwood Act of 1913. Thus we came to World War I with a moderate set of import duties, which, had peace been maintained, would have led to freer and more extensive world trade. But the war and its aftermath altered the situation violently.

The Republican administration in 1922, under President Harding, put through the Fordney-McCumber Tariff Act, which raised the tariff duties on an average from about 27 per cent to almost 40 per cent. And this was done at a time when the world was hanging in the balance as to whether trade was going to be freer or more restricted. The tremendous economic power of the United States was such that our taking high-tariff road forced the whole rest of the world—England, France, Spain, Italy, and most other countries—into a series of tariff rises. Then came the depression of 1929, and the response of the United States again, this time under President Hoover, was the Smoot-Hawley Tariff, which raised our tariff rates to an average of over 50 per cent. It gave us one of the highest tariffs in the world and forced a second round of tariff raising by all the countries of the world.

In other words, we, as the most powerful country in

the world after World War I, twice raised our tariff duties in such a way and to such a height that we forced the other countries to follow suit. When the Smoot-Hawley Tariff bill had been passed by Congress, practically all the reputable economists in the country, to the number of a thousand, signed a petition to President Hoover saying in effect, "Please, for the sake of the country, for the sake of the world, for the sake of international trade and for the sake of world peace, don't sign that tariff bill." It is an amazing feat to get a thousand economists to agree on anything, for they very rarely do agree. Yet in the face of such startling unanimity among the experts, President Hoover signed the tariff bill. *Clod*

Such was the American contribution to free trade and world peace. We set the stage for the tariff wars, the tariff building, the throttling of world trade that took place in the 1920's, and then we did it all over again in the 1930's.

It is arguable that a high tariff was a sound policy for America in the nineteenth century. The old infant-industry argument probably has some merit. But it is not arguable that a high tariff was a sound policy for us after 1919. I remember once talking to a manufacturer of chemicals. He was telling me with great glee that we could manufacture bulk dyestuffs that were sold by the ton and lay them down in Basle, Switzerland, and sell them more cheaply than the Germans from just across the border could sell their dyestuffs there. I said to him, "That's a very impressive achievement. But why do we then need a high tariff on chemicals? Why do we have to shut out the German goods if we can compete with them so successfully in Switzerland?" He replied, "We couldn't get

95

along for a minute without the tariff. Free trade would ruin the great American chemical industry."

What he meant was that he could not make such high profits in the home market without a protective tariff to shut out foreign competition. Actually his thinking was out of date, for by 1919 we had become a creditor nation; the whole world owed us money. Europe, for example, owed us some ten billion dollars in war debts that we said we wanted paid. We even insisted on being paid. We wanted principal, and we wanted interest, and we wanted payment every year. But how was Europe going to pay us? It could not pay us in gold because it did not have enough to pay any substantial sum. It could not pay us in goods because we put up the tariffs against its goods. It could not pay us in its own paper money because paper money from France or England or Italy was useful only in those countries, and if we could not use it to buy goods with, it was of no value to us. In other words, we said to Europe, "Pay us." And then went on to say, "We will not accept payment in the only way you can pay, that is in goods."

There was one thing that did help a little; that was the American tourist trade. During the 1920's hundreds of thousands of Americans went to Europe. I can remember in the summer of 1929 walking down the Rue de Rivoli in Paris for two blocks without hearing a word of French spoken, because the sidewalk was crowded with American college students there, who were talking English. But even the hordes of tourists could not take enough American dollars to Europe to enable the Europeans to pay their debts to us. A very odd situation resulted. We insisted on being paid, and we were paid, during the 1920's, about half a billion dollars a year. And how did we get paid? Where did Europe get the money with which to pay us? The answer is simple. We lent Europe about half a billion dollars a year. We lent the money through private channels and then Europe paid us through public channels, but we were getting paid with our own money. In 1930 we stopped lending, Europe stopped paying, and the whole world slipped into the chaos of the great depression. Just at that same time, to nail down the coffin lid on all hopes for freer trade and economic recovery, we passed the Smoot-Hawley Tariff Act.

Two illustrations will serve to show the kind of mental processes that lay behind the Smoot-Hawley Act, which helped to plunge the world into the dismal thirties and the economic difficulties that led eventually toward war. These are two true illustrations of how America was thinking at that time and the kind of arguments that we used.

One has to do with a group of silk manufacturers, largely from New Jersey, who went down to the congressional hearings on the tariff. They were asked what was wrong with the silk industry, which was in a very depressed state and had been in trouble even before 1929. They were asked what was wrong with the manufacture of silks, and they replied by saying in substance, "The trouble with the silk industry is this. Very high tariff duties were put on by the Fordney-McCumber Tariff of 1922. That meant that there were high profits in the silk industry, and this led all the silk manufacturers to overexpand and make more silk goods than could be sold in our markets. Then prices slumped and we lost our profits, and the industry is now in very bad shape."

The congressmen asked, "Well, what do you want us to do to help this situation?"

The reply of the silk manufacturers was, "Raise the tariff duties."

In other words it was the high tariff duties of the Fordney-McCumber Tariff that caused the trouble, and the only cure the industry could suggest was to raise the tariff again.

But an even better illustration and the one I like best of all from those tariff hearings was that of the apple growers of the Northwest. Now, the apple growers of the Northwest did not want a tariff on apples. America grows the best apples in the world. We grow apples as cheaply as anybody does. Nobody imports any apples into this country. There was, therefore, no question of a tariff on apples. But what the apple growers asked for was a high tariff on bananas, on the theory that if bananas were made sufficiently expensive people would no longer eat bananas, and if they did not eat bananas, then clearly they would eat more apples.

It was reasoning like this that lay behind the Smoot-Hawley Tariff. And it is typical of what we did in the period after World War I when we washed our hands of world responsibility and said, "We are going to live unto ourselves. We are going to live in splendid economic isolation. We are going to shut out the goods of the world and make our own goods for ourselves. What happens to world trade or to other countries is not our concern."

We, therefore, have a considerable responsibility for the economic chaos of the thirties, which led toward World War II. You must not forget that the depression started here in this country in 1929 and communicated itself gradually to the rest of the world. In Germany, Hitler's vote had been slipping badly until the depression came and economic insecurity brought him more followers. Indeed, much of the political disorder in the world was a result of basic economic disorders.

After 1934 the United States made a valiant effort to remedy some of the conditions it had created. The Hull Reciprocal Trade Treaties enabled our government to reduce the tariff rates without congressional action. We did actually reduce the tariff rates considerably and slowly whittled them down to an average of 35 per cent. Now in a new postwar period, just this last November at Geneva, we have negotiated a new series of trade treaties, which have reduced our tariff duties on the average to about 20 per cent. We are back where we were a hundred years ago with a low tariff.

Without introducing any element of political bias, it is possible to point out that as regards the tariff the Democrats have a better record than the Republicans, for, on the tariff, history is clear. The Republicans, since 1850, have made six major tariffs; they have raised the tariff five times and lowered it once. The Democrats have made four major tariffs since 1850. They have lowered the tariff four times and raised it none. The last reduction negotiated in November, 1947, was by a Democratic administration. In fairness it should be said that the lessons of the period after World War I are now so clear that a Republican administration would probably have negotiated something like this new reduction, had the Republicans been in power. But that is not certain, for there are still forces in the Republican party that, blinded by tradition, support a high-tariff policy.

The Geneva agreements, of which I spoke, are one of the most hopeful signs for world peace visible in a discouraging postwar period, and I am sure that you would all agree that it is discouraging. These Geneva agreements, in which we took the lead, do point a way back from the economic isolation of the 1930's to a world in which people trade in a friendly fashion with each other and more or less freely. By the agreements we promised not to raise the duties on 78 per cent of our import trade, and we made tariff cuts ranging up to 50 per cent. A few samples will serve to show the kind of reductions we made in our tariff rates effective January 1, 1948: Butter—14 cents a pound, cut to 7 cents; beef—6 cents a pound cut to 3 cents; whisky—$2.50 a proof-gallon, cut to $1.50; fancy leather—30 per cent, cut to 15 per cent; aluminum—3 cents a pound, cut to 2 cents a pound; fine silks—45 per cent, cut to 25 per cent. There are many, many more since the reductions affect 3,500 different items.

Moreover, every time we make a tariff cut in a negotiation with England, or with France, or with some other country, it applies to all the other countries. For example, if we make an agreement to cut the duty on Scotch whisky in part of our trading with England, it also cuts the duty on any Scotch-type whisky that comes in from Canada or any other country. In other words, these tariff cuts are general for everybody. This is so because we have treaties with most countries that contain a clause called the most-favored-nation clause, by which we promise to treat each of these countries as well in our tariffs as we treat that nation to which we give the most favorable terms.

We did not give these concessions for nothing. In return we got tariff cuts on our goods from twenty-two other countries. They promised, in addition, that as soon as they could they would drop their quotas and their other restraints on trade. The nations agreed in general to try to get along with as little trade restriction as possible, to trade more freely. And there are some experts who feel that this general commitment is more important than all the diplomatic negotiations that go on and even than some of the things that the United Nations is trying to do. There is some basis for such a feeling since people who are trading freely with each other are likely to establish and develop friendly relations. Freer trade makes for more general prosperity. And prosperity makes for peace. But (and the "but" is an important one) these trade treaties that we have just negotiated, and that have just gone into effect, are only to last for three years—until January 1, 1951. After that they can be modified or even done away with. It will take at least three years to get the world trade restored. Even if the Marshall Plan works, it will be a long time before Europe is sending us much and before we are selling them much. We will *give* them a great deal in the interim, but by the time true trade is started, three years will have passed, and at that point the binding quality of the new treaties will be over, and they will be subject to change or abolition.

Now, what disturbs many people as they look ahead is this: We are now in a period of inflation and high prices. What if we have a depression in 1950, if trade declines and business slows down? Then many will argue that we must protect the home industries and that we must protect them by raising our tariff. The argument for a tariff is very simple, very direct. It will be said, "We pay high wages. We charge high prices. We can't compete with the cheap labor of Europe. We must have a tariff to protect our labor, our industries, and our standard of living."

Anybody can understand that, and it sounds persuasive to the workingman as well as to the manufacturer. The fact that it does not work that way is, of course, much harder to explain. But one illustration will serve to show the actualities that lie behind the arguments.

In the period of the 1920's and 1930's the most highly paid labor in this country was in the automobile industry. We paid wages in that industry which were not equaled anywhere else in the country. They were equaled nowhere else in the world. And yet there was no country that could sell automobiles in competition with us. In other words, if a country is efficient and makes a good car and makes it on a large scale, there is no need to worry about the competition from low-wage nations. We could compete with countries that paid half the wages we did because we had more productive labor and a more efficient system of manufacturing. The rest of the argument that nations need to trade with each other—that everybody is better off under a system of freer trade and that such a system makes for world peace—is much more complicated, but its validity is unchallenged by objective students of the subject.

If we come to 1950 and we are in the midst of a business depression and if we have at that time a president like Mr. Taft, it is perfectly conceivable that the Republicans will once more raise the tariff and once more miss the chance of building up world trade, world friendship, and world peace, through freedom in commerce. I mention Mr. Taft, not because I do not admire him in some respects, but rather because it happens that his views on the tariff are somewhat more backward than those of his father and would be roughly appropriate for the time when McKinley put through his tariff in 1890. Since Mr. Taft has not yet passed beyond the 1890 stage in his thinking, it is more than we should expect that he should mature sixty years in three. Yet he certainly *might* be our next president; he might have a Republican Congress. And in the face of the next depression he might very well, as Hoover did in 1930, throw away our chances for world trade and world peace by raising the tariff.

Now, it is very hopeful that at Havana at this moment twenty nations are negotiating among themselves to create what is called the International Trade Organization, or I.T.O., which is trying to implement the trade agreements of Geneva by drawing up further agreements as to how countries may trade more freely with each other. I cannot but believe, with the experience that we had between the two world wars, with the facts of history staring us in the face, and with the responsibility that we bear as the most powerful economic unit the world has ever seen—I cannot but believe whatever the administration and whatever the conditions of prosperity or depression that we will not try to maintain this freer trade and work for peace and prosperity by removing the economic barriers that separate one nation from another.

Detlev W. Bronk

NOT SO LONG ago an editorial appeared in the *New York Times* entitled "Secrecy and Science." It pointed up the dilemma of which scientists and statesmen have been increasingly conscious. How do we assure the free dissemination of scientific information and at the same time suppress knowledge in the interest of military safety? No issue is more paramount or calls for more wisdom in its solution.

Detlev W. Bronk, president of Johns Hopkins University since 1948, is a specialist in physiology and physics. His contributions have been in the area known as biophysics. As chairman of the National Research Council, his responsibilities have been with scientists who direct scholarship on a national scale, and who therefore influence statesmanship in determining the shape of scientific progress during these crucial years.

SCIENCE SHAPES OUR LIVES

by Detlev W. Bronk

SCIENTIFIC DISCOVERERS have the characteristics of youth: curiosity and zest for adventure, the desire to learn and to understand, and a lack of respect for authority. These are the qualities that have led young men to explore the universe in which they lived and have brought men from the cave to modern cities and from barbarism to modern culture. At a time when science plays a part in every human occupation and shapes the features of our life, every citizen should understand the social role of scientists and science.

This view is now distorted by the recent march of men armed by science, by the blast of an atomic bomb. From such events has come a new awareness of the powerful influence of science on civilization. But with that awareness there is mystical respect for and unreasoned fear of the motives of science.

Science is no new force in human life. Science has been the concern of men since men first sought for knowledge, sought the ways of putting knowledge to human use. For man has always lived under the threat of destruction, against which science has been his most powerful weapon. Plagues have been an ancient enemy, made doubly dangerous because the attacking forces were unseen. The unpredicted forces of the elements walked in fierce solemnity to all who voyaged on the sea. Salvation has stalked his human prey and made men slaves to unremitting labor. Today science holds the promise of freeing men from such deaths and such dangers and of freeing the minds of men from the fear of unknown natural forces. Through science we have taken the world in our hands, and only the cowardly and the foolish will refuse to learn how to use it or take thought as to what we shall use it for in the creation of a new world.

I was literally awakened to such considerations early one morning several years ago. As the plane in which I was journeying came into Cairo for a landing, the flight steward rudely shook me out of sudden slumber. I glanced out of the window of the plane and there saw, stretched across the desert sun, the shadows cast by the three great pyramids as the sun rose. And here was a remarkable contrast, for there below me stood the symbols of the accomplishments of science in a great age of civilization. But these tombs had been erected for the glory of dead kings by the toil and labor of a thousand slaves. And I, on the other hand, had come in the space of two short days across an ocean and a continent without toil or labor, wrought by the development of modern fuels and internal-combustion engines and the science of aerodynamics. And here was new freedom, freedom for men to use as they saw fit, freedom from toil and ignorance and restricted labor.

The next day in the same journey, we left Cairo early in the morning and passed over the ancient land of Palestine. And there, along the shore and stretching back, one saw the green and fertile fields, feeding men as men had never been fed on that land before. Here again was a great contribution of modern science. But again one wondered for what purpose was it being used, for strife was going on in the land, even in those days.

And the following morning, as is the uncomfortable custom of the Army Air Forces, we took off from Teheran before the break of dawn. And as we jeeped out to the airport, I felt a curious striking contrast between the advance of modern science and ancient civilization. As we approached the landing field, a long train of camels came across the road. And as their leader with a tinkling bell faded into the distance, a Russian plane (made in the United States) glided down across the train of camels and landed on the field.

Within a few short hours we had left the ancient land of Persia and had come into the modern city of Baku. There one saw industry dedicated to the satisfaction of man's needs and man's desires. But here again I ask you, "What does man do with the achievements of modern science? Is it to gain a better life or to gain some undesired power?"

Finally, to finish the journey on which I had started, not many weeks later I came into Munich and found an old friend of mine working at his science amid the bombed ruins of the University of Munich. The challenge of a scientific civilization cannot be escaped. Man's curiosity and man's desire will lead him on into new fields of knowledge. But what we do with the accomplishments of science is for you and for me to decide. That scientist working there amid the ruins of Munich personified the human instinct to understand and control the forces of nature. He represents the men of all ages who have sought truth and understanding. He represents men who have sought new knowledge amid the dangers of strange lives and have withstood the hardships of poverty and the torture of the inquisition, as he had withstood the tortures of the Nazis. He personified, if you will, men who have faced a challenge of human ingenuity to explore the unknown laws of nature.

I would like to persuade you that science is one of the great adventures of the human mind, that it is not merely the occupation of a few with special training. But before asking you to agree with me on that, I shall tell you why I think a scientist does the things he does.

His first motive is curiosity. This instinct has led men of all ages to observe natural events, such as the movement of the heavenly bodies and the properties and behavior of animate and inanimate objects. But curiosity has driven men on with a desire to see that which was not obvious. And so, after the description of the workings of the universe had been accomplished somewhat, we find men dissecting the living bodies and plants and the human structure, in order to find out how the objects of nature are created. But even that quest had finally come to an end through the necessity for inventing instruments that extend the range of human resources, to see what man with his unaided eye alone cannot see, and to hear what the ear alone cannot hear, and to measure what the two hands alone cannot assess, and to feel that which no human sense has ever felt. And so Galileo invented a telescope to see into the heavens. And through the telescope, on the very first night he used it, he discovered the satellites of Jupiter and the mountains on the moon. And not long thereafter he observed heavenly phenomena that showed for all times that the earth is not the center of the universe and gave to man a new place of humility in the space in which he lived. And a man, looking at the structure of the human body or plants, desired to see more than the eye alone could see, and so there was developed the microscope, which made it possible to see structures that had not been seen before. And so from those days to this. On Mount Palomar in California there is being erected a great 200-inch telescope, which will permit men to probe into the heavens a million light-years away; and in the town of Princeton Vladimir Zworykin has invented a microscope that will magnify objects one hundred thousand times, using not light, but huge invisible electrons, which make their pattern on a photographic plate. Thus man has been able to see not only the structures of living things, but has been able to trace down the enemies of man, so that through Dr. Zworykin's microscope it is now possible to see and follow the viruses that cause influenza and many other diseases.

But man has still not been content in seeing beyond the limits of human sight. He has had the urge to look through objects through which light cannot pass. And so X-ray devices have been perfected that enable men to investigate interior structure of metals and living bodies and follow vital processes. Ernest Lawrence with his giant cyclotron has given to protons such enormous acceleration and velocity that, charging into atoms, they reveal their interior structures, the structure that no man has ever seen.

Using such devices, my colleagues have been able to map the course of those messages which relate the human body to its surroundings. For coursing under the nerves that connect the organs of your senses, your eyes, and ears, and the sensitive terminations of your fingers with your brain, there are minute electric currents, and it is these currents that report to the brain the condition of your surroundings and enable the brain, by mysterious processes, to integrate these actions into the response which brings you into proper relationship with your surroundings, enables you to flee a danger, or to remove yourself from an uncomfortable environment. These electric currents could not be detected by ordinary means, so it has been necessary to transform them into movements of a beam of light, which may be photographed and seen by the human eye.

In all of this, there is still the motive of curiosity and the desire for exploration. That, and a little more. Michael Faraday, for instance, working in the basement laboratory of the Royal Institution, passed an electric current through one coil of wire and found that, as it started and stopped, the current was induced and caused to flow in another coil of wire quite removed. He did not think and did not hope that he was starting the great modern electrical industry, which is the basis of the Associated Gas and Electric, and the General Electric, and the Electric Bond and Share, and all of these great corporate structures of American business that supply us with what have come to be considered vital necessities of life. And Gregor Mendel, working in the garden of a monastery, by the chance occurrence of different kinds of peas, did not have the hope that he was founding the modern science of agriculture. As explorers these men could not know where they were going. They were merely satisfying the urge for exploration. And it is these explorations of pioneers that have shaped our modern lives.

The scientist's second motive is a bit more difficult to explain, but I think it can be stated as the desire to bring order out of chaos. Curiosity impels a scientist to seek new facts through observation and experiment. But the natural **human tendencies of getting meaning out of observations,** of bringing various observations and facts into an ordered pattern are the great motives of the scientist. And there are a few who have had the supreme satisfaction of suddenly understanding the relationship of facts, of seeing how mathematical law can be formulated.

Charles Darwin had worked for years observing the variations of animal forms. He realized that he was dealing with observations of great moment, and he was faced with baffling inconsistencies. In his famous diary he writes, "I can remember the very spot in the road while seated in my carriage that the explanation came upon me to my great joy." To bring order out of chaos and attain understanding is one of the great satisfactions of the scientist's career. In such understanding lies not only his satisfaction but one of the scientist's greatest social contributions. And that brings me to the third of the reasons why a scientist does the things he does. That, I would say, is a desire to be socially useful.

The greatest social value that a scientist contributes is that which is least understood. It is the aesthetic joy that he gives to life by adding an understanding of natural phenomena and a liberation from ignorance and prejudice. He is one with all artists, such as the poet and the sculptor and the musician. And in giving joy he gives new meaning to life.

Here I want to remind you that the most useful of these values are usually derived from what is known as "useless research." We speak of man's conquest of nature. But it is not a conquest of nature. It is a greater power that men have acquired by virtue of their understanding of natural laws, which enables them to predict natural events, such as the course of weather; or enables them to control natural forces according to no laws, such as the flow of electricity through a circuit to light our lamps or run our motors; or which makes possible the control of epidemic diseases; which, finally, enables us to relate ourselves better to our environment. No man has conquered through science the heat of the summer and the cold of the winter. But by the laws of heat we have been able to develop air-conditioning systems and to build power plants, which we are now constructing for the better heating of the rooms in which you can better isolate yourself during the cold weather. And this brings me to one of the important facts of science. Man, through his understanding of nature, has been better able to adjust himself to his surroundings. What is the real purpose and use of the machine age, which has been made possible by science?

One of the memorable experiences of this war was to stand in the great court of Trinity College, Cambridge, and watch the flying forts return as one stood there in the neighborhood of Isaac Newton's room. Their silhouettes, blending against the soft English sky, seemed to proceed slowly because of their great height, moving one with admiration for man's mechanical genius that has driven his machines into the skies against the force of gravity, first defined by Isaac Newton as he stood there in that same great hall. A little later one would find, in the gathering dusk, that the fortresses were roaring down the runways of their scattered fields, and the machines became revealed as mere instruments of human crews. Waist gunners sat casually at their openings, waving as they passed. Bombardiers were in their transparent cages. Pilots taxied their ships to rest. They were men returning from a mission made doubly hazardous by enemy action and the dangers of an environment unnatural to man. They were the crews who made the majestic armadas of the air a symbol of man's new freedom from his natural limitations, gained by courage and by science.

The history of aviation is a long record of man's desire to gain that which he had not possessed, by a natural process of evolution: freedom from gravitation to move in three dimensions, swiftness of action, and great maneuverability. But what happened as man gained these new powers through science is typical of what so often happens with scientific developments. For as men went higher and higher, driven by their curiosity and sense of adventure, they soon reached the limits of their human powers, until, finally, in 1862, two Englishmen, Lasher and Coxwell, went to a reported altitude of more than twenty thousand feet. But at that altitude Lasher became unconscious and both of them would have perished had not Coxwell, paralyzed as he was, seized the valve cord in his teeth and, by nodding his head vigorously several times, succeeded in releasing the gas and coming down. On his descent he made this memorable statement: "I certainly shall not take it upon myself to set the limits of human activity and indicate the point, if it exists, where nature tells, 'You shall go no further.'"

Here is the true spirit of the explorer, the true spirit of the scientist who was not bound by superstitious regard for the forces that had brought about unconsciousness. The solution of this mystery was soon found by a French physiologist who discovered that in these higher reaches of the atmosphere there was not enough oxygen to maintain the action of the structures of the brain. In the last war considerations of strategy and tactics required that in our bombing of the Nazis' European forces we should fly at altitudes of twenty-five and thirty thousand feet, and men could not go so high unless they were supplied with instruments that gave them oxygen in accordance with their needs. So man, having gained one set of new powers through the use of science, found himself unable to use them to their full extent, because of other natural limitations, and so science had to come and solve another problem and make possible the use of the modern airplane.

Another characteristic that was much desired was the ability to move at high speed and to change direction quickly. The metallurgists and engineers worked for years to develop new materials and new motors and new wings that would make this possible. When they succeeded, it was found that men could not fly the planes they had created, for unconsciousness rapidly followed when they turned in sharp circles. And again, biologists, working with physicists and engineers, discovered that the blood was being forced away from the brain during these turns. I cite these instances to indicate that each new scientific development gives man new powers but also places new limitations upon his use of the powers which he has gained.

Science frees men, it is true, from the hazards of ignorance. But science and technology also create a complex civilization that taxes the capacity of the individual citizen. Each new scientific discovery that provides men with new powers creates new dangers. Modern industry creates a vast flood of material goods, but the machine worker of mass production does not enjoy and know the light of creation.

You would expect me, as a scientist, not to suggest that we abandon science. For even those who deplore most loudly the evils of our machine age are seldom heard to admit that they would be willing to go back to the days of an age that was not colored by science, go back to ceaseless labor and hardship and disease and lack of transportation and communication. The better life can be gained by greater use of science. This is a theme that Louis Mumford, great architectural critic, defines as the biotechnique civilization of the future, which furthers in particular the interests of the human body and the rights of man.

I must go on to say that the material contributions of science alone, no matter how directed they are toward the interests of human life, cannot create a rich and a satisfying existence. Nor do I believe that the intellectual values of science alone provide the spiritual satisfactions that men crave. Scientists are merely partners of many others in mankind's great endeavor. Science liberates men from the fear of unknown forces, frees men from grinding toil for mere survival, subdues pain, cures sickness. And in doing so, science frees men to enjoy art and music and literature, the beauties of nature and religious faith. Science makes possible the enjoyment of much that science alone cannot give. The social and the personal problems of today are part of a scientific civilization, and science must be used in their solution.

The reason why I have stressed repeatedly what science alone cannot do, and how science links our lives at every turn, is because it is only through a combination of science and the other forms of human occupation that we shall create a better life. And as you go out into whatever profession or occupation you choose, it is important that you realize not only the potentialities of science, but its limitations; that there is an urgent necessity that, as humanitarians, the lawyers and the engineers and the bankers and all of those who operate the machinery of life must work in conjunction with science. Science is not an end in itself.

This is a point of view that is receiving wide national recognition at the present time, for it is felt that scientific effort must be increased in the public interest. At the present time one finds much talk of the shortage of scientific man power. Such a realization of the fact that we are not training enough men to operate our present civilization has given rise to broad programs of scholarships and fellowships, which may run as high as twelve million dollars a year in federal funds. And I see in this movement the danger that is a threat to the unity of human activity, for too many men of ability are lured into the sciences. We may not have enough to co-operate with the scientists in creating a better world which can lie before us. Yet there must be a realization that trained man power is needed in the sciences, the humanities, in the social sciences, and in the arts: it is our greatest national resource, and must be found and must be trained and must be wisely used.

Also there is a growing recognition that through modern research we can deal with many of the urgent problems which now face us. And so one finds the National Infantile Paralysis Foundation and the American Cancer Society and the American Society for Mental Hygiene and others carrying out large campaigns abundantly supported by popular funds and the support of modern scientific undertakings. But not content with that, the nation is now considering in the present Congress a number of bills for the creation of a great national science foundation, which will support research in all fields, again, recognizing that the trained scientific man power and scientific knowledge are among the greatest of our national resources.

But these are movements that are not entirely whole-some. As I have indicated, the great movements in science that have most affected human life are those which have come out of pure exploration carried out with the spirit of freedom to seek where the curiosity leads. As scientists be-come more important, I foresee that they will be more nearly controlled and more frequently driven to do those things that seem to have an immediate practical purpose. But if we make haste quickly, we will not lay the founda-tion for a long period of growth and development, founded on basic scientific discoveries, such as those of Newton and Faraday and Pasteur and Mendel. Our own Willard Gibbs, working as an obscure professor in Yale University, laid the foundation for much of our modern chemical industry, merely by doing what he wished to do and following the whim of his own curiosity.

And finally I come to the point that science, while it shapes the lives of all men, is hardly a part of the lives of many men. Although we all live by the fruits of science, there are few who understand its motives, its purposes, and its accomplishments. And in many broad areas of the world, science scarcely impinges on the life of the people at all.

Now this has several serious consequences. In the first place, it makes it possible for individuals to gain control of vast power. They can control the scientific efforts of a trained personnel in a group of people or a nation. And furthermore, it makes it possible for certain nations pos-sessed with scientific resources to become great and mighty at the expense of others who have not been so wise in their support of discovery.

We must bear in mind that science, like nature, to which it belongs, is limited by neither time nor space but belongs to the world and is of no country and no age. Scientific discovery made in Warsaw or London is just as useful to citizens of Paris and New York. And the cure for a disease found in Moscow or Chicago will be just as useful as though it were made in Philadelphia. Science knows no boundaries, and yet, because of power that science gives to nations, there is a present danger that there will be a heavy restriction put on the freedom of scientists. This is not only of concern to the scientists, but it is of moment to all those who use science and all those who have a concern as to what science may do.

This was recognized by a great American statesman and scientist. Benjamin Franklin, writing in the year 1779, addressed this document to all captains and commanders of armed ships acting by commission from the Congress of the United States of America, which was then in war with Great Britain. The directive reads thus:

> Gentlemen. A ship, having been fitted out from England, before the commencement of this war, to make discoveries in unknown seas under the conduct of that most celebrated navigator and discoverer, Captain Cook, an undertaking truly laudable in itself, of increase of geographical knowledge, facilitates the communication between distant nations in the exchange of useful products and manufactures and the extension of arts. Whereby the common enjoyments of human life are multiplied and augmented, science of other kinds increased to the benefit of mankind in general, this then, is to recommend to you that in case the said ship should happen to fall into your hands you would not consider her as an enemy, nor suffer any plunder to be

made of the effects contained in her, nor obstruct her immediate return to England.

Had we more statesmen who possessed such a sincere and practical basis for internationalism, it is reasonable to hope that the affairs between nations would run a more wholesome course. Were there more scientists and scholars who possessed faith in sense of social responsibility, such ambassadors might be more numerous.

There are many causes of war and I am neither wise enough to define them nor foolish enough to consider myself capable of doing so. But certainly there is one that is presented to the peoples of warring nations. That is the necessity for more material possessions and a greater supply of food. Science offers today the power of gaining by peaceful means those possessions which they have heretofore sought by armed aggression. So science offers the hope of a more peaceful world in the contributions it can make to the desires of men. Science offers more than that. For it offers an understanding of the significance of nature and the unity of men and through its true spirit of internationalism can pave the way for a better world. Or to cite the Preamble to the Charter of the United Nations Educational Scientific and Cultural Organization, "Since wars begin in the minds of men it is in the minds of men that we must construct the defenses of peace." And as science shapes the minds and lives of men, it has the power for giving men the things they desire. Our great need is to see that men of imagination and devoted spirit shall work with the scientists to direct the contributions of science to worthy ends.

During the sixty years of your life's expectation, for science will make it such, you will see strange things come to pass. Now you will have gained the power long before you are deceased to do vast undertakings of which you can now not dream. Of this I have no doubt. For that I have no concern. My one concern is that you shall direct the course of science and its achievements so that it may bring man to a better estate and multiply all these good things that man desires.

Howard Thurman

IN 1946 Howard Thurman left his chair of professor of religion at Howard University in Washington to found, and serve as copastor of, the Church for the Fellowship of All Peoples, in San Francisco.

He has devoted his life to interracial problems. His reputation among educators furthering the cause of better human relations is international. Recently he delivered the Ingersoll Lecture on Immortality and Religion at Harvard University.

This essay, with its remarkable analysis of the place of fear and hypocrisy in the scheme of things—and their final exorcising—has its beginning in Augustine, Aquinas, and Calvin. The conclusion is his own—very new in expression, very old in tradition and truth.

THE RELIGION OF JESUS
AND THE DISINHERITED

by Howard Thurman

I T WAS IN the fall of 1935 at the beginning of a five-and-a-
half-month pilgrimage of friendship from the students
of America to the students of India, Burma, and Ceylon, that I was invited to talk at a law college at the University of Colombo on civil disabilities under states' rights in
the United States. Having no legal background, I suggested
that I would talk to the students against the background of
my own experience as a layman and leave it up to them to
translate, or transform, my words as a layman into jargon
that appealed to the legal mind.

At the end of an hour's discussion, the principal of the
law college invited me downstairs to have coffee. We drank
our coffee in silence, and when the service had been removed, he said to me, "I had not planned to ask you this
question, but after listening to you upstairs, I am convinced
that you are an intelligent man. What are you doing over
here? Oh, I know," he said, "what the newspapers have said
about the pilgrimage of friendship from the students of
America to the students of India, Burma, and Ceylon. But
that does not answer my question. What are *you* doing over
here? This is what I mean," he said. "About three hundred
and seventy-two years ago, your forebears were taken from
the western coast of Africa as slaves by men who were
Christians. The name of one of the famous British slave

vessels was *Jesus*. One of your famous Christian hymn writers, Sir John Newton, who wrote, among other things, the hymn 'How sweet the name of Jesus sounds to a believer's ear, publish glad tidings, tidings of peace,' made all of his money out of the slave traffic. You were sold, in the New World, to other men who were Christians. And for more than three hundred years Christian ministers, quoting the Christian Apostle Paul, gave the sanction of religion to the system of slavery. Seventy-two years ago you were freed by a man who himself was not a professing Christian, but who was the spearhead of certain political and social and economic forces, the significance of which he himself did not quite understand. For seventy-two years in the New World you have been a part of a Christian church that has insisted upon those forms of separateness and segregation all within the confines of a Christian fellowship. And now," said he, "here you are, in this land, talking with me, a Hindu, against that background and as a part of that tradition. I do not wish to be rude to you," he said, "but I consider you a traitor to all the darker peoples of the earth, and I wonder what you can say in defense of your position inasmuch as you are an intelligent man."

Our conversation lasted for more than six hours. The summary of what I had to say to him is, at once, the essence of what I have to say here.

In my thinking about the religion of Jesus in this connection, it will be abundantly clear that I am regarding Jesus as religious subject rather than religious object. I am regarding Him as one who was an experiencer of religion, rather than merely regarding Him as one who is the object of religious devotion. Any creative thinking about the religion of Jesus and His significance at this point has to begin with the simple historical fact that as Jesus lived in Palestine He was a Jew. As a Jew in the Greco-Roman world, He was a member of a minority group within the Roman Empire, a minority group that had lost its political freedom and with reference to the all-important fact of Roman citizenship it was a disinherited, and to that extent, underprivileged, minority.

Not only was Jesus a Jew and a member of a minority group within the Greco-Roman world, but He was also a poor Jew. As a matter of fact, He was so poor that when His family presented Him at the Temple when He was eight days of age for the Jewish ceremonial, they were unable to sacrifice a lamb at that time, in accordance with the Deuteronomic Law, but rather they were compelled to take advantage of that extenuating clause in Deuteronomy which insists that if a family be too poor to purchase a lamb for this important sacrifice, then such a family is at liberty to purchase turtle doves. When we read about the dedication of Jesus, as found in the Gospel, it is very instructive to remember that at the time of the ceremonial, His family used turtle doves.

In addition to this fact, the first great creative interpreter of the Christian religion, the Apostle Paul, was also a Jew. But, unlike Jesus, the Apostle Paul was a free Jew. That is to say, he was a Roman citizen with the prerogatives of citizenry. By blood, background, religion, training, social orientation to his environment, he belonged to an underprivileged Jewish minority in the Greco-Roman Empire. But as a result of a political, or economic, or social accident, or incident, he was a free Jew. Which meant, you see, that the ordinary limitations and proscriptions that obtained for Jews like Jesus at that time did not apply to Paul, even though by blood, background, religion, and training, he was one with them.

This very suggestive and significant fact altered in a rather profound manner Paul's philosophy of history. For instance, it was Paul the Roman citizen who said, "Slaves, be obedient to your Masters, for this is right in the Lord." It was Paul the Roman citizen who said, "All government is ordained of God." It was Paul the Roman citizen who said that the Christian should have the same attitude toward the civil magistrate that the Christian should have toward Jesus Christ.

Here was a man, you see, who, in a very subtle but significant manner, found himself inclined to go north and south at the same time, or east and west at the same time. If a Roman soldier were whipping Paul in some dungeon in Asia Minor, he could say to the Roman soldier, "Take your hands off me! I am a Roman citizen, and I appeal to Caesar." It is to the amazing influence of the spirit and the mind of Jesus Christ on his life that, according to the record, he used this thing only one time, but always it was there as a kind of threat, as a potential defense mechanism behind which he could retreat as a Roman citizen if his plight as a member of the Jewish minority became unbearable. But if a Roman soldier pushed Jesus of Nazareth into a Palestinian ditch, he could not appeal to Caesar. He was not a Roman citizen. Therefore, he was not protected by the normal guarantees that went along with Roman citizenship.

It is for this reason, then, it seems to me, that as Jesus thought profoundly about the meaning of religion and the meaning of the Kingdom of God, He was sure that the goals of religion could not be worked out within the limitations of the established order. And He thought of His Kingdom, in truth, as being not of this world.

Religion then, as Jesus experienced it, in the light of this analysis, was for Him and all of the other persons in the Greco-Roman world, thus circumstanced, a creative technique of survival for a limited, proscribed, disinherited minority within the broad expanse of the Greco-Roman Empire. Therefore, when Jesus, against that background, counsels with people who find at a particular historical moment that they stand with their backs against the wall, his words have a telling power that might not be quite true if those words came from the lips of Paul; despite the fact that there is in Paul the great affirmation of universalism that we quote again and again—that in Christ there is neither Jew nor Greek, bond nor free, and so forth.

There is an old Zulu proverb that says: Full belly child says to empty belly child, "Be of good cheer."

It is only the empty belly child who can say to the empty belly child, "Be of good cheer." Jesus, who stood nineteen hundred years ago without the protection of citizenship in the Greco-Roman world and with the stigma of a limited and proscribed minority, speaks to all peoples across all the years who stand at that particular point in their particular civilization or age.

There are two crucial problems that people who stand in society with the backs against a wall must face constantly and persistently. One is fear. Fear is a hound of hell that dogs the footsteps of the weak in any civilization, in any culture, in any period. And it's a significant kind of fear. It is not the fear that one has of a mouse, for instance. You react to that fear spontaneously, and it has an effect both on you and the mouse, and then it's over. But the fear of the disinherited is a climate, it is an atmosphere, that closes in on them and walks beside them wherever they go and whatever they may be doing. It presides over every fundamental decision that they make. All of their dreamings about the future and the possible fulfillment of life for themselves and their kind are under the aegis of this fear. It is not a fear of death, as such, for all men, soon or late, accommodate themselves to the fact of death. One by one the duties end; one by one the lights go out. We all know that. But it is the fear of violence that carries a death potential. It is the constant possibility that without notice, without warning, without any preparation whatsoever, there may descend upon one stark, naked violence. It is not the sort of thing out of which martyrdom is made, you see, because there is something glorious about dying on the wings of a great cause, a going out in triumph, moving on the crest of a wave of a tremendously significant moment in life, or history, or destiny. But it's the possibility of dying without benefit of reason, without benefit of a cause, without benefit of a purpose, but dying like a dog in an alley.

This fear has a very amazing effect on the personality. I'm not sure that I can put it into words. Our study of the anatomy of fear and the sorts of chemical changes that go on in the body under the threat of fear reveals that fear tends to express itself when it grips an individual, or tends to cause an individual who is gripped by it to express himself either in flight or fight.

But for the disinherited flight merely means being hunted, tracked down. The story of Europe reveals that all over again, to refresh our minds. Fight means to be overwhelmed, to have one's essential manhood pushed down and leveled out so that there is a deep sense of a profound loss of self-estimate, self-respect, self-dignity resulting therefrom. So that the fear, then, unable to fulfill itself either in flight or fight, flattens out within the organism until it becomes a small, curdling despair.

In addition, it has a very profound effect on the children. Children are taught how to behave so as to reduce the possibility of a mindless exposure to anonymous violence. They commit to memory ways of behaving that are automatic.

If I may illustrate the principle in another area, to revert to experience in India once again, the first night in the subcontinent, a very gracious friend came over to give us advice about how to survive in the country—certain precautions about food, and so forth; all of which we had, but he wanted to be sure. Just before he left he told us about the precautions with reference to cobras and Russell's vipers, those rather interesting but deadly snakes. He said, "Always sleep with a torch under your pillow—a flashlight under your pillow—so that, if for any reason during the night you must get up and walk around, you can describe a circle of light on the floor before you put your foot down, lest you may disturb the nocturnal ramblings of some unsuspecting cobra and then suffer therefrom. Don't walk around out of doors at night without a flash," he concluded.

After he left, I sat in my chair, and I was reminded by Mrs. Thurman that it was time to retire because the next day was a full day. I asked her if she would give me five minutes more. She said, "What are you doing?"

I said, "I am making my body commit to memory ways

of behavior with reference to what has been told us about the cobras so that after tonight it will not be necessary for me to refer to my mind in a formal and discursive sense to get action on these matters. Automatically, I will not walk out of doors without light. I will not get up without making a light on the floor."

Now that is precisely the thing that has been happening through all the years and is still happening at this very moment with all peoples who stand at a particular moment within their culture or civilization without the normal guarantees that go along with citizenship.

The religion of Jesus, then, addresses itself to this fact. Fear is a form of life insurance for the disinherited. And the words of Jesus growing out of his background are these: "Fear not. Fear not those who kill the body. And after that, there is nothing more that they can do but fear God." The insistence is that a man is God's child.

Now, we have said that so much, in our faith, that the utterly amazing significance of the insight is lost. But it has a particularly striking and significant word to the disinherited, because it directs itself at once to the stabilizing of their egos. It causes them to be internally convinced that the estimate that is placed on them by their highly charged environment is essentially false, and it engenders, in ways that I cannot quite analyze, a peculiar sense of inner relaxation and poise, which, in turn, makes it possible for them to lose their fear of other human beings. They recognize at once that fear of other human beings who are feared in the same category that God alone occupies. And it becomes, in the act itself, a radical form of blasphemy and, as such, is rejected on behalf of a new and creative orientation to their fellows. Under such circumstances men lose their fear, and even death becomes to them an insignificant and minor thing.

There is a second aspect to which I shall give about seven minutes, and then I'm through. The second hound of hell, as I shall call it, that dogs the footsteps of the disinherited, is hypocrisy. Hypocrisy is one of the oldest defenses of the weak against the strong. I have two daughters, and, of course, they know that I represent the power of, how shall I say it, the power of the State. They cannot oppose me in an open arena. I am the strong. They are the weak. But what do they do? They create all kinds of devices, beautiful, clever, innocent devices, that finally get me so involved that I do their will as if it were my own.

It is a thing that my students did when I was a teacher. They knew, for instance, that I was partial to any news in the magazines or the daily press about India, and if the going was very difficult, some innocent fellow would ask for a comment, or had I read a certain thing about Mahatma Gandhi. I would become involved at once in talking about it, and before I knew it, the bell rang, and the period was over. Everybody was saved.

It's an old technique of the weak against the strong. I've seen little birds in Florida in the meadows, when they saw the shadow of a hawk on the ground, take their little feet full of dried grass or leaves and do a quiet somersault, and the hawk, thinking he had an optical illusion, could go on his way to find some birds that didn't have sense enough to play dead. It's an old technique.

In the Old Testament, the prophet Ezekiel, giving comfort to the Judahites in the Babylonian captivity, described the King of Babylon, but he did not name the King of Babylon. He named poor old Hiram of Tyre. And the Babylonian Secret Service couldn't do anything to him, but all the Judahites knew he was talking about the King of Babylon. It's an old technique of the weak against the strong.

The one technique that has been tried effectively and successfully through the years has been the technique of deception. Don't fight the strong; fool the strong.

And Jesus, coming out of that sort of situation, which He had to face every day of His life, says that deception is wrong. Is deception wrong, even when deception means that you can save a life? Does deception become moral because a life is at stake? He says, "Let your words be 'Yes, yes. No, no!' "

Is He assuming that there is no fundamental distinction between the God of life and the God of religion; that the God of life and the God of religion are one and the same? He who acts in his given situation with a thorough-going honesty makes perhaps one of the supreme discoveries about life, namely, that there are some things in life that are worse than death. And one of those things is to deny one's own deep sense of personal integrity, even at the risk of the loss of one's life. What would a man give in exchange for his life, for his integrity?

Was Jesus right, or was He insane? With that kind of madness He established a fresh, creative meaning to the commonplace drab miseries of the lot of the majority of the human beings in any age and in any civilization. And His religion shall never be able to claim the world until it demands of men what He discovered—that each man is a child of God, that the grounds of one's integrity must never be invaded by deception even at the cost of one's physical existence. What a challenge! What a high road!

> I saw a man pursuing the horizon,
> Round and round they sped.
> I was disturbed at this.
> I accosted the man:
> "It is futile," said I
> "You can never . . .
> "You lie," he cried and ran on.

Lewis Perry

IT IS MY surmise that no school teacher in America has ever been more widely known or deeply loved than Lewis Perry, who served as principal of Phillips Exeter Academy from 1914 to 1946. "Lawrenceville," he remarked in the preamble of his address, "has always meant a great deal in my life, for I came to Lawrenceville from New England as a boy of thirteen. It was there that I began teaching: an act of fate, mingled with the gambler's instinct on the part of the Head Master, which seems to me now to have been amazing."

In the essay that follows you will see expressed the ripe wisdom of one who has helped shape the destiny of three generations of boys, and you will feel the import perhaps of his conclusion: "We laymen must be the foundation on which will be laid that great structure, a hopeful and a peaceful world, a vision of a future fit for man."

T. H. J.

A LAYMAN LOOKS AT
HIS WORLD

by Lewis Perry

SCORES OF HAPPY memories come back to me as I again
see Lawrenceville in the springtime. Here the world
looks so clean and fresh, and hopeful, and ready to
begin life all over again—at least, nature's part of it—and
you can't help but think that if man's part in this world
only kept up with nature's part, we would not have to
worry about war and the preparation for war.

As a columnist said the other day, "As I look around the
country there is one thing that gives me hope as we seem to
be drifting into war: the American people." That's our
greatest wealth, our fine, wonderful, generous people.
France and Italy are full of the same kind of warmhearted,
friendly, eager people. The funny thing is that, despite all
the propaganda and the Iron Curtain between us, I'm sure
that the Russian people are exactly the same way if we can
only get by their rulers. They get sentimental over cherry
blossoms; they get worried about the future; they don't
want their children to get into another war. If we could
only reach them and they could reach us.

As a layman, I would like to have a conference with you
later and see where we stand on matters of supreme importance, the most important political matters that have
come up in the history of the world. You will not agree
with me, necessarily, nor I with you, but we belong to that

great body of well-disposed persons who hate war and long for peace. We long for peace all over the world, and we find ourselves drifting toward war. We seem to be in a trend that is almost irresistible, and struggle as we may, we look upon ourselves as hopeless heroes in a Greek tragedy. Fate and the opposing forces are too much for us.

I imagine that we are all laymen. We get our ideas from the experts who guide us in our thinking. And we have good guides. The ordinary layman gets his information about world affairs from different sources: the columnists, the radio speakers, clergy, politicians, and from conversation. Remember, I am giving just the idea of one layman. I'm not expressing ideas which are necessarily true or necessarily important. I read what certain columnists say with great interest, and from their words I get information of light and leading. But in my case there are very few which are downright helpful. The best ones, in my judgment, write for such dailies as the *Times* and the *Herald Tribune*. I think we come down a few pegs when we listen to the regular radio speakers. They have very little time, they have to catch our attention, and they must be dramatic. This, at least, is true of the majority.

On listening to the radio one has to be careful not to swallow too much propaganda. Most of the men who speak on the radio do not have special sources of information. The information is fed to them from a central office and they feed it to us. But one could listen to the radio interminably without acquiring much wisdom.

The politicians won't do much for you in an election year. I'm talking about the politician who wants your vote. I'm not talking about such men as Senator Vandenberg, or Leverett Saltonstall, or Christian Herter. We want knowl-

edge. We want to acquire wisdom. In general, we won't
get it from the politicians.

The editorials in our great dailies are our best source of
information. Nor will we get world knowledge from the
clergy. They rightly feel that they can help us more in
spiritual ways, and the clergyman is naturally, and rightly,
shy about expressing his political beliefs.

I suppose we get most from the books we read, the lectures we hear, the conversations in which we engage. Lucky
is the young man who has the chance to sit in on good
conversation. The opportunity for this is much greater at
Lawrenceville now than it was when I was a schoolboy. The
inquiring young man knows far more about his world than
we did. In fact, our ignorance of world affairs was nothing
short of abysmal. But we had something that is open to us
now and that to me is of the greatest importance: we could
read history. History will make you understand the fundamental fallacy in Hitler's ambition to rule the world. It
will make you understand—as nearly as anything can make
you understand—what is working in Stalin's mind. Study
of history will give you the basis of the later study in college
of philosophy, and of politics, and of religion. Here, it
seems to me, is an all-comprehensive subject for us laymen.
For eventually we are the ones who must decide which way
we are going, and our voices must be heard.

Coming down on the train today, I had the opportunity
to read the first installment of Winston Churchill's life. He
says it's not history. He says that he is writing it too soon
after the events to make it history. But it's written in that
wonderfully clear, incisive style which makes you think of
Macaulay. If you want a little introduction—some of you
boys who may not be taking history courses—to history, read

it. It's coming out in the *Times,* it's coming out in *Life,* these installments of Winston Churchill's life, marvelously entertaining and marvelously instructive.

But you can go on to read what history you can in the summertime, for I really believe that, if we are going to decide the questions we've got to decide within the next ten years, we've got to know more history than the average layman knows. We must think for ourselves as clearly as we can and without prejudice. For critical practice on your part I will give you one layman's views on a few burning questions as he looks at his world.

This layman knows from experience that there are a great many other laymen with as good a background, or better, who do not agree with him. He believes that Russian expansion must be checked. There's no doubt that the United States has got to increase its military strength. He is therefore in favor of strengthening our army, navy, and air force. We are told that this necessitates more research, universal military training, the draft, and greater air force, in order to give military support to the recently formed Western European alliance. To have to do all this within three years of victory is profoundly discouraging. The United States cannot afford to let Russian totalitarianism exploit our weakness. He believes that at the moment firmness and strength are less likely to result in open war than continued weakness.

I do not like the advice of those opposing a strong policy. In my judgment they are not advising us well. When Henry Wallace says we should get together with Russia and talk peace, what does he think we've been trying to do for two years? What papers does he read? The record shows that despotism, whatever its form, has a remorseless tendency toward aggression. This was true of the Kaiser, of Hitler, of Mussolini. History shows that four times we have waited too long to preserve the peace. Four times. With the Kaiser and the invasion of Belgium, with Mussolini and the invasion of Ethiopia, the Japanese invasion of Manchuria in 1931, Hitler's first tentative steps in the Ruhr.

Today another great and despotic power threatens to extinguish freedom in Europe. One cause of World War II was the misapprehension of Hitler as to the real intentions and the will to fight of the free, democratic nations. He was confident that what he had been told was true, that the United States was weak and would remain weak. We wish, today, to make our determination clear.

August 22, 1939, Hitler said to his commanders-in-chief, "We've nothing to lose; we can only gain. Our enemies are men who are below average; no personality, no men of action. Our enemies are little worms. I saw them in Munich." Nine days later the Nazis marched in open war against Poland. Today the issue of civilization, no less, depends upon the United States. The wonderful, reluctant giant is making progress but not enough. Great numbers of our people now see that we must lead if we are going to survive. But this revolution in our thinking has been an intellectual revolution to a large extent. It has not seeped down into the consciousness of the great mass of the people. As long as legislators think of themselves as delegates from their districts rather than as representatives who lead, the policy of the United States will continue to move by fits and starts.

First knowledge we laymen should have is the knowledge of what we are up against. One of the foreign policies of Moscow is to retake those objectives Russia would have achieved if she had been among the victorious powers at the Armistice of 1918. As President Truman has said, "The Soviet Union and its agents have destroyed the independence and democratic character of a whole series of nations in Eastern and Central Europe." It is this ruthless force of action and the clear design to extend it to the remaining free nations of Europe that have brought about the critical situation in Europe today.

Now we are no longer aquiescent. We are resistant. And so, supporting the Russian demand for the veto right in the security council, we deferred to the request that Russia be given three votes in the assembly of the United Nations. Now we see the spirit of expansion, which, throughout history, has always troubled the souls of the Muscovite leaders.

How strong should we be? Strong enough, says the *Times,* to make war unprofitable for anyone else. This is the best guarantee of peace that there can be in today's world. So I've come to certain conclusions. The number-one foreign policy of the United States must be to establish world peace. We must have a strong military policy. Whether we like it or not, the United States is the leader of Western society, and from Western society must come the leadership for peace. It's time for a showdown on this business of organizing the world for peace. But it does no good to have Russia a member of the United Nations, which does nothing. Moreover, it is better to have a showdown on a matter of principle, such as the future of the United Nations and the survival of civilization, rather than on something like a boundary dispute.

What I should like to know is this (perhaps some of you can tell me): Does Russia want more territory or does she merely want to spread communism through the world? If she wants more territory it may mean war; if she merely wants to spread communism, it probably does not mean war. My guess is that in the complex Russian mind, there is a little of both desires. So I am for a balanced strength in war power, on the ground, on the sea, and in the air. An air force capable of seeking out and destroying the enemy that might impose war. A navy capable of defending the necessary sea lanes of the world from submarine attack. An adequate army. I'll leave the number here to the experts, but I would like to use the wisdom of General George C. Marshall, who seems to me to stand out, not only for his knowledge but for his integrity, a truly great man.

In addition this layman naturally favors the Marshall Plan. To me it is the great, generous spirit of modern times. When we made the loan to Great Britain there was a great deal of haggling, backing and filling, we weren't satisfied; England wasn't satisfied. Before we got through what really was a dollar at the start was worth about sixty cents. Inflation had ruined whatever generosity we might have had. But now, for once, without long debates in Congress and without saying those terribly unpleasant things about the nations whom we have helped, we have given all these nations a chance to start over again, get on their feet and go forward. I pray that nothing may hinder this Marshall Plan, which is more than just lending money, more than giving encouragement to nations; it's a great moral and spiritual boost to the world. I, for one, am proud of that.

In contrast with rearmament, this is a positive program. It gives hope to people who still wish to remain free. Communism flourishes on fear and despair. Men fear to oppose it openly lest they mark themselves for liquidation. Desperate men also stand for communism, believing in its fraudulent promises of betterment. So the United States will bolster men's courage to resist. The European relief program will inspire their hopes. This, very briefly, is what I believe the present United States' foreign policy to be, and I support it as far as it goes, for I believe that, for the moment, it lessens the chance of war.

Fundamentally, however, this is a tragic policy, for it accepts the division of the world and merely seeks to strengthen our side. In the long run war is almost inevitable with the world divided into two armed camps. Great effort must be made to bridge the gap. The present policy of rearmament and alliances must be supplemented by a genuine and fundamental plan offering some long-range hope of peace. As Mr. Churchill said on January 23, "The best chance of preventing war is to bring matters to a head and come to a settlement with the Soviet government before it is too late."

The problem is to find the basis for such a settlement. To provide such a basis, a plan of settlement must hold out such great hopes and be so appealing to the people of the world that even the Communists will have difficulty in opposing it. At the same time it must in no way weaken the power or will of the free people. In fact, it should inspire them to greater belief in the rightness of their own way of life.

I would suggest (and here I lose part of my audience, I know), I would suggest that world federation be given consideration as a basis for such a settlement. By "world federation" I mean, briefly, a United Nations with an assembly in which all nations are fairly represented. Not only on the basis of population, but on the standing, productivity, and influence in the world. This legislature should have power to make laws gradually substituting a world police force for national armaments. It should also have the power to levy taxes, but it would not have the power to deal with money or trade or immigration or the social, religious, or domestic affairs of the nations. Powers would be much more limited than the powers of our federal government. In short, its fundamental law would be that all disputes must be settled without fighting, and it would be given power to enforce that law before war occurs—not afterward, as at Nuremberg.

If this became the ultimate objective of the United States' policy it would inspire great hope in people all over the world. It would also put the Soviet government in the very unhappy position of having to choose between joining the world federation or facing a unified, noncommunist world. Such a policy involves great risks and may not succeed, but are these risks as great as the risks of war? And in the decisions that have to do with the future of the world, the teachers, the writers, the musicians, the businessmen must all play a great part. There have been four great periods in history: the Age of Pericles in Greece, the Augustan Age of Rome, the period of the Renaissance, and Elizabethan England. In each one of these periods the writers and thinkers, the producers, in other words, the laymen, have had great influence in contributing to a great age.

In these dark days for the world I firmly believe that America's great age is before us. It will take courage and patience and wisdom to bring it about. We surely have the courage, possibly the patience, and we must pray to God for wisdom. You and I, I mean. Wisdom in ourselves, wisdom in our rulers is not enough. We laymen must be the foundation on which will be laid that great structure, a hopeful and a peaceful world, a vision of a future fit for man.